D1116699

Communes in the Counter Culture

COMMUNES IN THE COUNTER CULTURE

Origins, Theories, Styles of Life
by Keith Melville

William Morrow & Company, Inc., New York 1972

Preface

Call it the "youthful opposition," "the Great Conspiracy," "Consciousness III," the "counter culture" . . . there are already dozens of names for it, fashions in these things changing as rapidly as the thing itself does. Is it still possible to say anything about it without being chased to the extreme position of either defending its every gesture or attacking the whole thing as mindless iconoclasm? I have the feeling that, as in any escalating battle, all the middle ground may be bombed out, that the two sides are digging their trenches. The only thing that can be said with any certainty is that in a conflict such as this one, in which so many basic values and assumptions are under attack, the issues aren't going to be resolved easily or quickly.

In the trenches on one side, the ossified defenders of the status quo. And on the other, those who uncritically celebrate the youth culture. There is no better example of this latter position than Charles Reich, who has somehow become a major interpreter of the younger generation to their elders with his book *The Greening of America*. Like Friedrich Schlegel's *Lucinde* (whose subtitle, "An Apology for Nature and Innocence," Reich might well have used himself), which caused the kind of sensation in 1799 that *Greening* has recently caused, Reich's book is a manifesto. It never attempts to sort out what is useful from what is not in the counter culture. In the process, it does a disservice to the young, who desperately need sympathetic but critical help in their program of building an alternative society. Reich's book sounds like a nominating speech, all hyperbole and one-sidedness, constantly soaring beyond the bounds of credibility into the rhetorical beyond. (Item: "Bell bottoms have to be worn to be understood. They give the ankles a special freedom as if to invite dancing right on the street. They bring dance back into our sober lives. . . .") Reich almost shouts out the message: *If elected,* Consciousness III promises to deliver everything that I and II before it did not.

Unfortunately, even though my sympathies lie much more with the counter culture than with the mainstream culture that it so energetically opposes, things are not quite that simple. I dearly hope that a number of the characteristics of this emerging counter culture disappear as rapidly as Hula-Hoops did; I feel just as strongly that some of the *other* ideas which the counter culture bears may provide absolutely necessary alternatives to American culture. There are in the midst of this debate a number of issues that must be critically examined. This kind of examination has very little to do with the conventions of scholarly analysis; it has even less to do with the exchanging of manifestoes.

Every once in a while a single issue lights up the whole social landscape, and that is what the youthful opposition has done. It calls into question the assumptions normally buried in social habits and institutions, and it illuminates many of the weaknesses of American culture. All new historical eras have this in common: There is a refashioning of reality. One of the best places to look in order to understand how reality is now being refashioned by rebellious young people is at the youth communes, these scattered outposts of the counter culture. To dismiss those who retreat to communes in New Mexico or Oregon as "drop-outs" running away from the problems of the real world is to miss the fact that valuable ideas are being tested in the communes. In the later chapters of this book, I examine several of these ideas and discuss their significance as cultural alternatives.

Despite the fact that the communal movement has been growing very rapidly during the past few years, the communes do not yet provide an "alternative society." Whether or not this movement continues to grow, and whether these groups that are currently populated by people in their late teens and early twenties expand to become real communities, remains to be seen. But even if they don't yet provide a *solution*, a true alternative culture for the young people who have left their pasts, they are a very good place to look in order to understand the *problem*.

I share Peter Marin's sense of inadequacy as well as his feeling of responsibility to help chart a path in this unfamiliar landscape, and can do no better than to repeat his words:

> As for me, an adult, I think of myself as I write as an observer at a tribal war—an anthropologist, a combination of Gulliver and a correspondent sending home news by mule and boat. By the time you hear of it, things will have changed. And that isn't enough, not enough at all. Somebody must step past the children, must move into his own psyche or two steps past his own limits into the absolute landscape of fear and potential these children inhabit. That is where I am headed. So these ideas, in effect, are something like a last message tacked to a tree in a thicket or tucked under a stone. I mean: we cannot *follow* the children any longer, we have to step ahead of them. Somebody has to mark a trail.[1]*

---

* All bibliographical notes will be found on pp. 241 ff.

Contents

1 : Introduction: The Uses of Utopia

Aaron sat on his haunches, tracing patterns on the ground, occasionally rubbing his hands on bib overalls covered with dirt from the field where he had been working. Looking vacantly through a scraggly beard and shoulder-length hair, he was remembering why he had come here. "I was living in Los Angeles, and every day I felt one step closer to cracking up and landing in a mental hospital, totally isolated from other people and their lives. Every time I turned on the tube, there was this very slick guy selling Miracle Formula 87 to save me from terminal halitosis. Like it was insane, it was a pressure cooker, and I had to get out. I racked my brains trying to figure out what I could do. I tried a shrink . . . no use, of course. Finally, I decided that I would have to live in the country and work closely with my brothers and sisters. What was there to choose from in the city? City life offered me a trivial job I didn't want, a prison, or a mental hospital.

"I came here because I wanted to simplify my life as much as possible. It wasn't hard to drop out. I had a lot of things to get rid of—a car, a hi-fi, a million useless things. I mean, why did I need an electric toaster and a coffee maker all my own? So I got rid of it all. It was like getting a good load off.

"I had done the political trip for a while, but I got to the point where I couldn't just advocate social change, I had to live it. Change isn't something up there, out there, and it isn't a power trip. It's in here." He thumped his chest twice, and little puffs of dust exploded from his coveralls. "This is where I have to start if I want to change the whole fucking system."

Aaron squinted in the direction of the lodge, where a dozen people were sitting, talking, doing nothing in particular. "This whole generation, all the people who are receiving these new energies and turning on, we don't want to be in the materialist bag anymore, and we don't want to get caught up in the nine-to-five career bag, the two-week vacation, barbecues-in-suburbia bag. We don't want these things because through successive incarnations we've been there. . . . If I was put on earth for anything, it was to love my brothers and sisters, and these other things just aren't important.

"It was my dream to belong to a tribe, where the energies flow among everyone, where people care for one another, where no one has to work, but everyone wants to do something because we're all mutually dependent for our survival and our happiness. So we got together here," and he waved his hand out over the garden and the mountains beyond, "and we've had a lot of problems and real conflicts, but we know the satisfactions of trying to work around them, of growing from them, the way you grow from a good marriage. And we're back to the land here, and like I get high just being close to the earth and trying to understand it.

"I think most people came here in the first place because it was a refuge. They weren't sure what to expect, but they had to escape. The new people come with their minds stamped with a thousand patterns that just don't make any sense here. But we're all learning new values, and we're learning how to live together. We still get hung up on a lot of bad trips. Everyone has his thing that's holding him back. But we're strong here because we know what we're trying to do. Like it's so obvious that civilization is doomed. I mean the whole thing's just going to self-destruct, and we don't want to go with it. The next step is community, and that's what we're trying to do.

"It's an entirely new evolutionary branch. The premise of all these places is that we love one another. And people have to experiment in order to figure out what that means. All the communes, all the families, are facets of the same thing, but no one knows exactly what that thing is, or what it should be, so we all go about it a little differently. . . . What we're really doing here is a pilot study of a life style for the near future. We're trying to slow down, to remember what this whole trip's about. We're simplifying, getting rid of all those things that just get in the way. We're retribalizing, and when we get it all together, the vibes are so high we know we're doing something right. And like so many people are getting turned on, it's the beginning of a whole new age."

Marx observed that the essential contradictions of any society are concentrated in the proletariat. In the nineteenth century, during the forced march of industrialization, he was right. But in our own time, the perverse logic of the affluence that resulted from the Industrial Revolution has reversed Marx's formulation. Cut in on the profits, the working class is docile and content, and confrontations between hard-hats and longhairs are only the most recent evidence that laborers have become the staunch defenders of the status quo. Now the central contradictions of the affluent West are the legacy of the young, who face them most directly because they are shopping around for a life style and are not yet committed, either economically or psychologically, to the status quo.

The contradictions are obvious enough. We live in an economy of abundance, but continue to make the assumption of scarcity. As Philip Slater recently argued in a brilliant essay about the strains in American culture, if we make the assumption of abundance, that the things that we desire are plentiful, then it makes sense that everyone should have them; sharing rather than hoarding makes sense; and the number of things a man accumulates is unimportant in determining his status. But we continue to make the assumption of scarcity, that human needs are satisfied only with great difficulty. Therefore it is appropriate for men to compete among themselves for scarce resources. The people who have accumulated the greatest number of things are the most "successful." Despite our rhetorical commitment to equality, we maintain economic inequality and defend it for its uses, as an incentive to others, and as a source of capital. Inequality is justifiable if we assume scarcity, but unjustifiable if we assume abundance.[1]

It is, of course, no small task to maintain the illusion of scarcity and its corollary, that the accumulation of material goods symbolizes victory over scarcity. The advertising industry is concerned solely with the task of heightening need, of creating a demand for new things and more things, however trivial. The traditional wisdom of the East has been that happiness comes only when the fires of appetite are banked; the wisdom of our economic system rests on the assumption that a market can be created for any new product, that our appetite for material goods is almost infinitely elastic.

That assumption is generally true. We are afflicted with the electric-toothbrush syndrome; the previously unnecessary very rapidly becomes part of our taken-for-granted

material world. Since so many of our material "needs"
are synthetic rather than natural, created by the media
rather than proceeding from our natural appetites, the
most extraordinary efforts have to be made to convince
us that our industry is indeed practical and not, fundamentally, an ingenious diversion. Eric Hoffer reminds us
that Hero's steam engine was used "to work tricks in
temples and divert people at banquets." [2] Despite the
protestations of scientists of a thousand different pedi-
grees, the suspicion remains that our newest rockets
and satellites—along with most of the other new applica-
tions of technology—are similarly fanciful, magical, and
playful tricks we are using to divert ourselves. They are
magnificent public relations, to be sure, but "practical"
only if we accept the tenets of the "crackpot realists,"
the myopic expositors of a logic fundamentally antithetic to
real human needs.

The assumption of scarcity generates the most seductive of vicious circles: Means become ends. Rather than
working only as much as is necessary in order to have
the things we need to be happy, we continue to work,
to accumulate. Compulsive consumerism reinforces the
compulsion to work. In a society that encourages its members to expend most of their energies in work, the defer-
ment of emotional gratification is prescribed, since it
counteracts both work and acquisition. The work ethic
condemns pleasure-seeking as an end in itself and sub-
stitutes a circular chain of utilitarian assumptions: Pleasure is limited to its instrumental value, as a necessary
respite from work in order that a man can be renewed
for yet more work.

In the affluent society, we applaud each new technological advance, assuming that each new step brings us
closer to the material Promised Land. Yet while we con-
gratulate ourselves on our ingenuity, we have never been
in the habit of asking what will be the total impact of

each new invention upon human life. Since our national genius has been to solve the problems that are amenable to technological or economic solutions, it never occurs to us that technology has its own imperatives; "the more, the better" has a hypnotic appeal. Thus it appears perfectly appropriate that the successor to a skyscraper billed as "the world's tallest" should be a building just a little higher. Both our economy and our national psychology are set against redirecting our energies. We have been trained to respond with approval to indexes of growth, which completely obfuscate the prior question of whether growth itself is desirable. To use Michael Harrington's phrase, ours is an "accidental century," plagued by unanticipated problems that technology has caused but cannot and will not alleviate.

Yet for every national problem, we are offered the palliative of economic growth, of improved employment rates, of higher per-capita income, and increasing Gross National Product. Economic and technological considerations take precedence over social and cultural claims. In a society that worships the idol G.N.P., it is heresy to suggest that the solution might lie in reducing our material needs, limiting consumption, and redirecting our efforts.

But our celebration of technology has more subtle and more serious consequences. As Gabriel Marcel said, it is easy to take up technics and almost impossible to put it down. For technology requires that man take on some of the characteristics of his tools, as well as vice versa. In a society dominated by technology, its logic—regularity which suppresses the idiosyncratic in favor of the predictable, the mechanization of time, the veneration of efficiency and output—stamps itself on the rest of the society. All questions are ultimately decided by the experts, men whose final appeal is to science. And aside from science, there is no truth. The claims of the nonra-

tional realm are distinctly foreign to this rational, em-
pirically knowable world of everyday experience which
is the dominion of science. Consequently, we live in an
age that has forfeited its responsibility to take seriously
the problem of meaning; our religious traditions are little more than hollow forms inherited from other eras.

As our assumptions become barriers between us and
our emotions, as they urge us to deprecate all the categories of the nonrational, they also cut us off from one
another. Alienation, the feeling of being isolated and
communityless, is something more than a modern catch-
word. For all our material prosperity, we have failed to
make a human environment in the cities; there is a continuing disregard for the primary bonds of community
and for the alienation caused by unmanageably large
bureaucracies. The legacy of several generations of ram-
pant individualism is the suburban house on its quarter-
acre lot, a symbol of inviolability, a self-contained unit
which obviates the need to be dependent on anyone outside one's immediate family. As Slater observes, "an
enormous technology seems to have set itself the task of
making it unnecessary for one human being ever to ask
anything of another in the course of going about his
daily business." [3]

In the midst of it, we feel a gnawing awareness of the
peculiarity of our plight, that we are the first civilization
that has been able to afford such splendid isolation. And
this is the most telling contradiction of all: that having
finally realized the affluence which had only been
dreamed of by men in other ages, we find that this system
that provides so efficiently for our material needs is fundamentally antagonistic to many of our deepest human
needs.

For the young who sense the seriousness of these contradictions, the task is nothing less than the creation of

a new community which serves the human needs that American culture now neglects or denies. And that is precisely where the counter culture starts: "Our purpose is to abolish the system (call it the Greed Machine, Capitalism, the Great Hamburger Grinder, Babylon, do-your-jobism) and learn to live cooperatively, intelligently, gracefully (call it the New Awareness, anarchism, the Aquarian Age, communism, whatever you wish)." [4]

If any movement so diffuse as the counter culture can be said to have a single point of origin, it began several years ago as a small group of insurgent youths with a specific list of grievances about unfinished national business—the social and economic condition of the American Negro. At the outset the tactics of radical pacifism were sit-ins and other acts of nonviolent resistance. In the years since, the movement's goals, tactics, and rhetoric have changed. Civil rights gave way to Vietnam protests and campus reform; massive demonstrations became the most prominent tactic; and the refrains of "Hell no, we won't go," and "Do not fold, spindle, or mutilate," succeeded "We shall overcome." In turn, dissent gave way to resistance, and the list of specific grievances was replaced by a catalog of American hypocrisies and failures.

In the process, what began as a coherent movement has become something that looks more than anything else like a mixture of all the elements. One part of the counter culture advocates violent change, another militant pacifism. One side advocates the eminently practical state of mind of radical politics; another the mind-blown state of psychedelia. Dionysian and frenzied on the one hand, it is gently contemplative on the other. At one extreme are the outspoken, the extroverted, and the posed; characteristic of the other extreme is a nearly catatonic reclusiveness. Its heroes are a strange congregation—Allen Ginsberg, Che, a Yaqui Indian named Don Juan, Lao-tzu,

Abbie Hoffman, Thoreau, Eldridge Cleaver. . . . What is the common chord in this cacaphonous mixture?

It is, I think, a movement that can be defined neither by its tactics nor its goals (both of which vary enormously) but by a shared sense of a common enemy. It is integrated by a refusal to share the dominant assumptions that are the ideological underpinnings of Western society. Slater summarizes its main features: "The old culture, when forced to choose, tends to give preference to property rights over personal rights, technological requirements over human needs, competition over cooperation, violence over sexuality, concentration over distribution, the producer over the consumer, means over ends, secrecy over openness, social forms over personal expression, striving over gratification, oedipal love over communal love." [5] In the counter culture, these priorities are reversed. In most respects, it sets the assumptions of the dominant culture on their heads and in the process becomes the most thorough contemporary critique of the established order. Even if the counter culture so often lacks coherence and unity, even if it is so frequently self-contradictory because it is a reaction against the ratified values of the mainstream culture rather than a coherent vision of what a viable alternative might be, it is much more substantial than a movement *pour épater le bourgeois*. Part of it does involve nose-thumbing at the sanctities of the mainstream culture. But in fundamental respects, it is an attempt to move beyond affluence, to resolve the festering contradictions of most of the Western nations. (According to a recent report, even the Soviet Union has its variant form of the counter culture, the "Bichi bands," consisting of "former bank directors, builders, disappointed artists, metal workers, graduates of circus schools and piano tuners," who travel in itinerant bands through the Russian hinterlands.[6]) In America, the most affluent nation in the world, these contradictions are glaringly obvious.

Yet despite its unity on one level, the counter culture is characterized by a very serious cleavage on another. This cleavage, as I argue in Chapter three, is between activists and hippies. The agenda of the political young reflects a concern for what Kenneth Keniston has called America's "unfinished business," an end to poverty, an end to the hypocrisy of the Vietnamese war and the consequent maldistribution of resources, and complete social and economic equality. The goals of young revolutionaries make sense to most Americans, for these goals are, after all, time-honored American tenets. Revolutionaries want power, and this quest for power is comprehensible to most Americans. Even the strategy of change through political revolution makes sense since Western history has been punctuated by such revolutions.

But the agenda of the apolitical young is almost incomprehensible in comparison. In the words of B. F. Skinner, it is the agenda of people who have chosen to let this culture alone and to establish one of their own. Their task is to create a society (if only a society in microcosm) that reflects the values and aspirations of the counter culture. Who are these cultural revolutionaries? More consistently than their political counterparts, they are white and come from affluent, middle-class families. They are the heirs to the American Dream, youths who were promised careers as doctors and lawyers, youths who had Mustangs when they were eighteen. This is the supreme irony of affluence, that having inherited the postindustrial society with all its material wealth, its beneficiaries reject its fruits and return to small, primitive, intentional communities; they leave suburbia and return to the land, glorifying folk culture, the qualities of the rural peasant, and the idiosyncrasies of ethnic minorities. And in "dropping out" in increasing numbers, they are rejecting the wisdom of Westchester and Winnetka.

Of all the characteristics of this counter culture—such as its stress on the importance of uninhibited self-expression and its desire to create an alternative to authoritarian leadership—its sensitivity to alienation of any sort is its most marked characteristic. Alienation takes the form of impersonal bureaucracies, of cities which overwhelm the possibility of dealing with people as anything other than obstacles or acquaintances, of role expectations (such as the student-teacher dichotomy) which impede personal contact.

In response, there is a thirst among the young for genuine encounter in any form. For example, the instant community of rock festivals. Or demands for a "campus community." In one of the most interesting documents of the counter culture, the catalogs of alternative universities, the desire for encounter is reflected in most of the course descriptions. These are some of the course offerings at Berkeley's Free University:

> *Turning on Social Systems:* Innovative opportunities for action in reforming, humanizing and revitalizing social systems.

> *People's Pack Party:* A small group of us will walk to one of California's purest high-vibe scenes. For seven days we'll get ourselves together, dig the vibes, let it be, and do whatever develops.

> *American Romantic Mythology:* . . . the bullshit of romantic love handed down to American youth by the culture in expectation of their achieving mature and relevant relationships. Working definition of romantic love and enlightened alternatives.

> *Gestalt Growth Groups:* For those willing to risk the change of growth, gestalt awareness through hot-seat work and gestalt experiments.

Massage: Valuable for increasing the awareness of civilization-numbed bodies, anti-body culture, and for the sheer pleasure of giving and receiving.

Judging from sheer proliferation, sensitivity-training groups appear to be the most widespread manifestation of this thirst for encounter. The norms of these groups set the tone for the preferred interpersonal style of the whole counter culture: The chief villainies are uptightness, cerebration, game-playing, and lack of spontaneity. The sensitivity-training group encourages spontaneity and the sharing of intimacies; the intensity of the emotion expressed is the most important thing about the encounter. Overlooking the faddishness of encounter groups, and the extreme belief that intense emotions and intimacies should be shared by people who are barely acquainted, there is something of underlying importance going on here. That is the genuine concern for breaking down the barriers between people, an intense effort at de-alienation.

Certainly the most significant expression of this quest for encounter is the creation of intentional communities that reflect the values of the counter culture. During the "flower children" phase of the hippie movement in 1966–67, even though San Francisco's Haight-Ashbury district held the honor of being christened by *Time* magazine the "vibrant epicenter" of the hippie phenomenon, there were similar regional centers throughout the country in such places as Griffith Park in Los Angeles, New York's East Village, Denver, Atlanta, and Chicago. During this period the life style of the urban enclave was tested and found wanting. At roughly the same time, the appeal of radical politics as the movement's primary tactic started to wane. The answer to both problems was to "drop out," to leave the city and search for both an alternative means of effecting social change and alternative life styles with a future. In 1967, Timothy Leary, more a popularizer of the "drop-out" concept than its originator, advised his following that "the leftist activists . . . are repeating the same dreary quarrels and conflicts for power of the thirties and the forties, of the trade union movement, of Trotskyism, and so forth. I think [we] should be sanctified, drop out, find [our] own center, turn on, and above all avoid mass movements, mass leadership, mass followers." [7] Thus at the same time that their activist counterparts were developing more violent techniques of destroying the old society, the program of the communal movement became the creation of a new society in microcosm.

The idea of forming intentional communities based on beliefs that are radically at odds with those of the rest of the society is an old one. In the last century groups such as the communes in Paraguay and workers' collectives in France, and after World War I communes in England, have been a common if intermittent feature of the social landscape. What is remarkable in this new communal movement is the number of people involved and the fact that the communes appeal so widely to the young. Disregarding the American communal groups that are fragments of other ideals and other eras, such as the Hutterites in North Dakota, there were not more than a handful of communes in this country in 1965. Since then they have been springing up like underground Howard Johnson's. Now there are at least a thousand.

But what is a commune? If one of the hallmarks of the counter culture is its diversity, diversity itself is certainly one of the characteristics of the communal movement. As in any discussion of the counter culture in general, the hardest task in discussing the communes is to distill common themes and features out of a wealth of details, most of which are unique to a particular group. Certainly there is no single model of community. The forms that communes take are often complementary but sometimes contradictory. Here is a sampler of six groups which indicates at least the range of different styles of communal living:

—The Ananda Co-operative, in the foothills of the Sierras, is a community of several dozen young people led by an American yogi named Kriyananda. As he has written in a booklet entitled *Cooperative Communities—How To Start Them and Why,* "to 'hie away' to the country, then, need in no way imply a rejection of one's social responsibilities. It can become rather the beginning of a sincere assumption of such responsibilities." From the precept that all good things come from the inner man, it follows that a "self-realized" man will be a force for good in the larger life of all men. At the Ananda community, self-realization is encouraged by the operation of a meditation center for outsiders. Two worship services are held daily. The community has prohibited the use of drugs and raises its own organically grown produce. Members share two large geodesic domes and several A-frame cabins in the woods.

—Just over the hills from Oakland, California, thirteen people live together in two large brown-shingle houses in a woodsy, countrified atmosphere. As members of Vocations for Social Change, their main activity is a clearinghouse for information, projects, and jobs. The radical ideas expressed in a monthly newsletter are disguised in moderate rhetoric ("so that we can speak both to *Life* magazine and the White Panthers"). Both housekeeping and financial resources are shared by all the members. There are weekly meetings at which each member talks about his own problems and experiences. As one member explains it, "We need to keep understanding where each of us is at, because if we didn't, we'd never be able to live together and care for each other twenty-four hours a day."

—Compared to the orderliness of Ananda and Vocations for Social Change, a group of several dozen high-school students in the Bronx that called itself simply "the family" lived a primitive and unpremeditated existence. Their home was a previously unused and garbage-strewn section of a park in the Bronx; shelter consisted of three huts built of sod and sticks. Several kids slept in the huts, while the other members congregated during the day. Predictably, "the family" quickly became an object of official concern. "Why, if we let them do this," said a spokesman for the Parks Department, "it could lead to a shack city." And although one police sergeant who was assigned to the demolition job reportedly referred to the huts with admiration as "bunkers," demolition was completed. Now defunct.[8]

—The Women's Collective in Berkeley grew out of a discussion group that met to share experiences and ideas about work in the Movement. The group currently consists of seven women, most in their early twenties. Aside from the responsibilities of living together, the Collective is held together by a shared concern for a wide range of political issues.

—TransLove Energies consists of three Victorian mansions in Ann Arbor's fraternity district and a rock group known as the MC5. The houses are used variously as offices, record rooms, bedrooms and dining rooms, media and communication centers, and band-practice rooms. In the words of

John Sinclair, a TransLove Member who was the founder of the White Panther Party, and has recently been sentenced to ten years for possession of marijuana, "We are a conscious community of artists and lovers who live together, work together, share all things—smoke dope together, dance and fuck together, and spread the word together every way we can—through our work, our freedom of movement, our music and dance, our economy, our human social forms, through our every breath on this planet." [9]

—Located at the top of a tortuously winding road on a mesa north of Taos, New Mexico, Morningstar East is one of the regular stops on the hip circuit of rural communes in the Southwest. The only thing that can be said with any certainty about Morningstar East is that the members (that is to say, whoever happens to be there) live in huts made from adobe bricks which are manufactured by the community, share a communal kitchen, and work the fields together. The life style is primitive —no electricity, outdoor "shitters." There is much drug use and a mystical orientation. Most of its faults as a community, as well as its virtues, are a consequence of its open-ended, anarchic style.

Certainly these six communes, and hundreds of others, are part of no single movement in any traditional sense of the word. The unity of the communes lies in widely shared beliefs about the functions that a community should serve, about community as a de-alienating context. Primitive man never had to face the problem of alienation. For him, the moral and institutional order were taken for granted. A strong sense of group solidarity and a feeling of naturally belonging to one's tribe reinforced the belief that whatever social forms existed—whether they were specific rituals, prohibitions, or traditions of family organization or tribal leadership—were sacred and unchangeable. Civilization changed all that. We pay the price of alienation, and we gain the sense of the possible, the revolutionary dream, the knowledge that society is a human creation arising out of specific social and economic conditions and can be changed.

This sense of the possible is an important part of the sensibility of the counter culture. It takes the form of demythologizing apparently fixed institutions and entrenched assumptions. Accordingly, any institution— whether monogamous marriage, a democratic system of government, or a capitalist economy—is viewed as a process. Here, as in Louis Sullivan's dictum in architecture, form follows functions. A social structure is judged not according to its durability, which is a dangerously inappropriate criterion in an era of rapid social change, but as a process which should serve specific human needs. In this sense, much of the best of what is happening in the counter culture is an attempt to topple outmoded assumptions and to resist institutional inertia. As Edgar Friedenberg has noted, "In many respects, our conception of integrity is outmoded; we include in it many ways of feeling and acting that acquired their social significance under social conditions that no longer exist. . . . Individualism, which led to success in a society dominated by the economic necessities of industrialization and empire, is a poor model for the young today." [10] It is on this level that the unity of apparently dissimilar communes becomes evident. They are attempts to create new models. They are different strategies toward the same goal, the creation of a community that serves basic human needs more efficiently than does the mainstream society.

If the program of the communes is to create a new life style, a society in microcosm, this ethos is best expressed by the rural communes. There are many urban communes, and "Resistance" communes very much involved with the task of evolving a hybrid style, consistent with both the exigencies of urban life and radical politics on the one hand and the need to develop new social forms on the other. But much less concerned about doing something about this society than their urban counterparts, the rural communes are freer to create a new one. The embracing of the anarchist tradition, a return to an intimate community, the rejection of technology and the materialist ethic, and the search for alternative nonrational realities are fundamental themes in understanding the counter culture in general. But, specifically, these are the themes of the embryonic new society being created in the rural communes of the counter culture.

Paul Goodman remarks in *Gestalt Therapy* that "the great task of anthropology is to show what of human nature has been lost and, practically, to devise experiments for its recovery." In many respects, this is exactly what the communes are, experiments for the recovery of human potential. In their eclectic gathering of cultural bits and pieces—combining Zuñi ceremonials and yoga meditation disciplines with Buckminister Fuller's geodesic domes and Esalen-developed group-sensitivity techniques—they frequently look like a class project in a freshman anthropology course. But they serve one critically important purpose: The commune movement is the most serious attempt to revive ideas and social forms which have been all but submerged. At their best, the communes are an attempt to raise new possibilities, to formulate an alternative society. To use a word which is held in disrepute by both young and old, the communes represent an attempt to define a *utopia*, to formulate a model of a society better than the existing society. To use Kenneth Keniston's definition, they are "an attempt to make imaginatively concrete the possibilities of the future." [11]

Utopian thinking in the nineteenth century was shaped by factors that seem very remote to us in the last decades of the twentieth. The Industrial Revolution generated the revolt of the working classes. Beginning with the promptings of self-interest, that revolt broadened into the socialist movement, which embodied a utopian vision responsive to the fundamental social problems of that era. The socialist vision included a new social order as well as the abolition of poverty. But utopia was one of the casualties in the rough transition between the nineteenth and the twentieth century. First victimized in the struggle between Marxist "scientific utopianism" and the other nineteenth-century programs for social reform, it was then doomed to pejorative usage by the failure of the Soviet experiment.

There is another fixture of the nineteenth century that seems even more remote than the hopes of the Socialists. That is the buoyant optimism which was the legacy of the Enlightenment, the belief that men are capable of discovering the truth and building communities that embody that truth. The schemes of Saint-Simon, Fourier, Owen, and dozens of others reflected the heady optimism of an era in which utopia seemed to be achievable. In America in the nineteenth century the extraordinary proliferation of communitarian experiments had few connections with the socialist movement. Rather, these experimental communities were an eminently practical means of effecting radical social change in a country and an era in which the shape of the dominant institutions had not yet been firmly established. The European utopias were mainly literary, theoretical things, or attempts to inspire men to revolution in order to usher in a new social order. In America in the nineteenth century, the communitarian movement was an attempt to test a hundred different conceptions of the ideal society in the crucible of a small community. In the next chapter, I discuss several aspects of this characteristically American attraction to intentional communities as a means of comparing the communes of the nineteenth century with those of the counter culture.

But we are all anti-utopian now. We have heeded Machiavelli's warning that "men make the mistake of not knowing when to limit their hopes" and so have foreclosed our sense of the possible. Nineteenth-century beliefs in the perfectability of man and society appear as naive to us as the simple-minded heroes of the Horatio Alger stories. The lessons we have learned are a distrust in idealism, a disbelief in the potency of rationality to guide men's actions and a fear of sustaining the foolish hope that a different and better society is possible.

One unfortunate consequence is that intellectuals, who created the utopias of the nineteenth century, have turned away now from the responsibility to generate ideals. In sociology, the founders of the discipline in the nineteenth century such as Comte and Saint-Simon generated images of what society might be. Since then sociology has become a discipline almost exclusively concerned with measuring and analyzing what is. Disregarding the utopian task of respecting what is while maintaining a concern for what might be, sociologists now dissect the corpse of social pathology. And create a science of the future, concerned not with what should be, but with the formulation of predictive statements about what probably will be. As David Riesman has commented, general cynicism about any assertion of what ought to be has its academic counterpart in the "value-free" attitude of the social sciences, the tradition of ethical relativism. As a consequence, "sociologists shrink from this [utopian] task; being 'in the know' as to a particular set of details, they are suspicious of the injudicious who make plans without such knowledge . . . and where scholars and men of superior intellectual training fear to tread, cranks and charlatans fill what market there is for big, bold, bad plans." [12]

Stripped of the utopian vision of the nineteenth century, we are pushovers for the merely technological utopia. During the period in which we have learned a thorough skepticism about man's ability to reorder his society, we have become firm believers in the limitless capabilities of technology to execute our most heartfelt (as well as our most trivial) material needs. The last century has taught us that, technologically, the impossible takes a little longer but is definitely attainable. So we have the World's Fair view of the future, a material Promised Land created by Union Carbide, General Motors, du Pont ("better things for better living"), and their corporate brothers. By the year 2000, we are promised, "the population of the world will have increased fourfold and stabilized, seawater and rocks will yield all necessary metals, knowledge will be accumulated in electronic banks and transmitted directly to the human nervous system by means of coded electronic messages, and genetics will allow the scientific planning of the personalities of the next generation." [13] Like little children in a toyshop at Christmastime, we know that however preposterous our request, it will probably be granted.

But where does this leave us? In the wake of the "end of ideology" debate, we realize that, as poverty has been lessened, socialism has lost its relevance as a vision of what our society might look like. But where is the utopian vision that responds to the problems of the twentieth century as socialism responded to those of the nineteenth? In a technological society that has no vision other than estimated growth rates and G.N.P. projections, how do we think about the future? In 1958, when most of the material promises of the American Dream had been met, President Eisenhower was persuaded to deal with the problem of national direction in the same way that most problems that are politically insoluble are dealt with— by the appointment of a commission of experts which dutifully produced a volume called *Goals for Americans.*

As Karl Mannheim said, we are "faced with the greatest paradox imaginable, namely, that man, who has achieved the highest degree of rational mastery of existence, left without any ideals, becomes a mere creature of impulses. Thus, after a long, tortuous, but heroic development, just at the highest state of awareness, when history is ceasing to be a blind fate, man would lose his will to shape history, and therewith his ability to understand it." [14]

To be sure, *utopia* has a new meaning and a new guise in an age in which buoyant optimism has given way to cynical "realism." As an attempt to define an alternative society, the communes of the counter culture have more coherence as a set of choices made to avoid the dystopian specter of the dominant society than as a positive program. But whatever their initial motivation and despite all their shortcomings, they perform the indispensable utopian task of providing a model of an alternative society, and showing "what of human nature has been lost." For all their distrust of any utopian blueprint such as B. F. Skinner's *Walden Two,* most of these young people who have chosen to live communally would agree with Skinner that "the successful design of an intentional community might be the most exciting and encouraging achievement of the latter half of the twentieth century." [15]

Utopia has always had two meanings. It is, on the one hand, the vision of a better society. On the other hand, utopia is illusory, a quixotic search in violation of what we know of human nature and Aristotle's rule that "in framing an ideal we may assume what we wish, but should avoid impossibilities." Like utopia, the communes of the counter culture have these two aspects. There is a good deal to be learned from each of them. What men search for, after all, is as important as what they find. It is at least a measure of their aspirations, their nature, and their unfulfilled needs.

2 : *"America Is a Utopia"*

"I am come to this country to introduce an entire new system of society; to change it from an ignorant, selfish system to an enlightened social system which shall gradually unite all interests into one, and remove all causes for contest between individuals."

—Robert Owen

The words quoted above were delivered by the English industrialist-turned-utopian entrepreneur in the Hall of the auspiciously named New Harmony community in Indiana, 1825. Owen's purpose—"to introduce an entire new system of society"—and the dream of a new harmony both strike a characteristically American theme.

To Europeans during the Reformation era, the American colonies held the hope of an earthly paradise. On this virgin land they would return to the essentials, make a new beginning, and work toward the regeneration of the world. Ever since, America has been a haven for idealists of every brand, as well as for adventurers and avoiders leaving unfinished business behind in hope of a better life. The remnants of this idealism are scattered throughout the land: New Haven, Connecticut; Equity and Utopia, Ohio; New Hope, Pennsylvania. In a very literal sense, the American continent represented the New

World. Alfonso Reyes, the Mexican statesman, is only one of the observers who has remarked that, in his words, "America is a utopia. . . . It is the name of a human hope." [1]

In this country, more than in any of the European nations, the utopian urge has frequently taken the form of small intentional communities. If America itself became something less than a utopia, then the solution was to detach oneself from the mainstream of the society and to band together with a small group of like-minded idealists to test some notion of the perfect society. During the eighteenth century, there was a series of experiments in communal living—the Labadists in Bohemia Manor, Maryland, the Ephrata colony in Pennsylvania, and the early Shaker villages, to name only a few. But compared with what followed, these were only bare beginnings. Both Owen and New Harmony were very much of their time, part of the ferment of nineteenth-century utopian thinking which attracted the eminent, such as Bronson Alcott, Horace Greeley, William H. Channing, and Nathaniel Hawthorne, as well as the unknown. During the first half of the century more than one hundred experimental colonies were started; in the second half of the century there were fifty more. This was a widespread movement which involved at least ten thousand men, women, and children.

For all the differences between these communal experiments of the nineteenth century and the communes of the counter culture, there are a number of fascinating parallels which make it worthwhile to glance back briefly before examining what is happening today.

Of all the attractions of the new continent, potentiality was its most alluring characteristic. In most societies, the institutional furniture is so thoroughly arranged that, short of the revolutionary task of destroying it all, there is an overwhelming sense that not much can be done, that—for better or for worse—all the important questions have already been answered. In the American colonies, and later on the frontier, there was the exhilarating feeling of making new institutions, of participating in the construction of a new society from the ground up. Most of the experimental communities were formed on the frontier in the early nineteenth century, in western New York, Ohio, Indiana, and Illinois. But even though these communities were located on the frontier, this was no frontier movement. Rather than people spontaneously banding together into communal groups in order to survive, as the Pilgrims at Plymouth had resorted to communism for reasons of expediency, this was a thoroughly idealistic movement. Communitarian ideas were planted in the East; most of the propaganda came from Boston and New York. Most of the communitarians were uprooted Easterners, middle-class idealists moving west for the land, freedom, and seclusion necessary for these experiments. Along with George Ripley, founder of Brook Farm, which was one of the exceptional groups located in the East, they hoped that "an association which would create but little sensation in the East might produce an immense effect in the West," still unformed and full of utopian potential.[2]

If these groups attracted retreatists interested mainly in the security of small socialist colonies, the loudest voices were those of zealous reformers, men possessed with the mission of restoring the earthly paradise. For example, Robert Owen and his Declaration of Mental Independence at New Harmony: ". . . with these *Great Truths* before us, with the practice of the social system, as soon as it shall be well understood among us, our principles will, I trust, spread from Community to Community, from State to State, from Continent to Continent, until this system and these *truths* shall overshadow the whole earth, shedding fragrance and abundance, intelligence and happiness, upon all the sons of men." [3] Such were the promises of New Harmony, the remodeling of society, and the remaking of the moral order.

But why the unprecedented interest in communitarian experiments during this period of the nineteenth century? The availability of the frontier is only part of the answer. There had been a frontier in the eighteenth century, after all, and only a handful of communal groups. A. E. Bestor, the most perceptive historian of the communitarian movement, has pointed out that one unifying theme among all these communities was the belief that a small experimental community could be used as a means of effecting radical reform. By the beginning of the nineteenth century, the individualist notion that the evils of the world have their source in some defect of human nature had eroded in favor of an alternative explanation, that evil resides in the social organizations which shape individual consciousness. Therefore, any effective reform must change those social forms. The convulsions caused by industrialization were so rapid and extensive that gradual reform was futile. But the prospect of effecting radical change through revolution was even bleaker in the wake of the European revolutionary experiences between 1789 and 1815. [4]

The alternative to revolution was to form intentional communities that embodied radically new ideas. In 1843, Albert Brisbane, one of the leading spokesmen for communitarian reform, argued the merits of this radical strategy:

> If we look around us, we see numerous Parties, laboring isolatedly to carry out various reforms—political, administrative, currency, abolition, temperance, moral, etc., etc.—which proves, *First,* the depth and extent of the evil that preys upon Society, and *Second,* the necessity of a fundamental reform which will attack

that evil at its root and eradicate it. . . . The reform
we contemplate, although fundamental in its character, is not destructive, but constructive; it . . . will
change quietly and by substitution what is false and
defective; it will violate no rights, injure no class . . .
but will improve and elevate the condition of all, without taking from any. It can, moreover, be tried on a
small scale, and it will only spread when practice has
shown its superiority over the present system. Unlike
political reforms, which to effect the smallest change
of policy agitate and often convulse a whole country,
and array one half of the People against the other half,
it will not affect a space as large as a township and but
a few hundred persons, and will not extend beyond
these narrow limits unless its advantages—*practically
demonstrated*—excite a strong and general approba-
tion in its favor.[5]

In many respects the forming of intentional communities was a means of reform particularly relevant to the
times. It promised radical and immediate change, if only
within the confines of a small community, without the
costs of revolution.

There is, of course, no single utopian tradition, no single list of ideas that characterizes utopian thinking. At
one time or another, utopian theorists have come down
on both sides of every question about how a society
should be arranged. In the nineteenth century, communitarian experiments tested a wide variety of different programs for man's salvation. Nearly every conceivable suggestion made in the name of reform received a hearing.
These communities were the bearers of many new ideas
which have since become standard items in the liberal
platform, such as abolition of slavery, educational reform, and equality of the sexes. And inevitably in a
movement which tested so many ideas, it was also a
showcase for the fanatic fringe. Faith healing, food cults,

experiments in eugenics, and various brands of spiritualism were all practiced at one time or another. Bronson Alcott refused to "enslave" animals by using them on his farm. And two Shaker girls were ordered to whip one another because they had watched "the amour of two flies in the window." [6]

Some of the communes of the nineteenth century were products of the tradition that most of the earlier experiments had grown out of, Christian communism. "And all that believed were together, and had all things in common; and sold their possessions and goods and parted them to all men, as every man had need . . . and did eat their meat with gladness and singleness of heart." [7] Several of these groups, such as the Rappites and the Zoarites, were isolated experiments which attracted many foreigners. More influential than any of the other sectarian groups, the Shakers established about a dozen new villages in the early 1800's and were important in spreading the communitarian ideals. Then, as the Shakers shifted their attentions from theology to social reform, they helped to bridge the differences between the religious socialism of the seventeenth and eighteenth centuries and the secular socialism of the nineteenth.

With the two great movements of communitarian excitement in the last century, as with so much else in the American tradition, we imported our ideas and put them to the test of Yankee practicality. The first of these was the Owenite movement which began in the 1820's, the second the Fourierist movement twenty years later.

Robert Owen, the British industrialist, and Charles Fourier, the French social reformer, were contemporaries. Both lived through the French Revolution and the Napoleonic wars. Both experienced the convulsions of rapid industrialization. Owen gained a personal fortune by successfully managing several mills in England and Scotland. At the New Lanark mills in Scotland, he was responsible not only for the factory but also for the village that surrounded it. Gradually his interests turned from factory reform to comprehensive social planning. As the benevolent autocrat of New Lanark, he tried to solve village problems as collective faults rather than individual failures. If there was crime, drunkenness, or unproductiveness, these were symptoms of social maladjustment, signs that something had to be done about the institutions of New Lanark. Accordingly, in his management of the village, he emphasized the importance of educational reform, of preventive rather than punitive control.

Owen's abilities in humane village reform were exceeded only by his genius as a publicist. In 1812, he began an active career as a pamphleteer, publishing a four-part essay entitled *A New View of Society: or, Essays on the Principle of the Formation of the Human Character*. First turning to legislative reform, he was quickly discouraged. Then, in 1816, he began to proselytize actively for immediate reform through the establishment of many small-scale communal experiments. A flurry of pamphlets followed, along with several communitarian newspapers—all propaganda directed primarily to the upper classes rather than the working classes. In 1818, he addressed international diplomats at the Congress of Aix-la-Chapelle; in the next several years, he spoke to various well-placed people in the aristocratic circles of England and France. By 1820, Owen had an international reputation, but, with the exception of several Owenite communities which had been proposed in Philadelphia, there were no experiments in sight. Then, in 1824, Owen came to America and sparked the communitarian movement. He purchased the village which the Rappite colony had spent ten years in building on the Wabash River in southern Indiana. In this ready-made village, christened New Harmony, he tried to put theory into practice.

During the decade in which Owen made his fortune,

Fourier lost his. Born into a wealthy family, he lost a large inheritance in the French Revolution, and spent the rest of his life as a timid bachelor constructing his own meticulously arranged cosmology. Had he been born in the fifteenth century, there would have been a happy coincidence of personality and historical era; he could have combined his childish imagination and an obsession for details as a chronicler of fables. But he had the misfortune of living in a country and a century which refused to indulge his fantasies. Fortunately for his reputation abroad, his writings—which contained a few genuine communitarian insights buried in a heap of chimerical speculations—remained untranslated. Thus the rest of the world was spared the sheer minutiae of his classifications of the Sixty Malevolent Characteristics which had made civilization a "sink of Corruption," and his "passionate series" of eight hundred types of individuals who comprised the facets of a full community, as well as dozens of other equally useful insights. How did a closet prophet like Fourier stimulate an unprecedented communitarian movement which began several years after his death in a country he never visited? Very simply. Albert Brisbane was a young American disciple of Fourier. In 1840, he published *Social Destiny of Man,* a distillation of the best of Fourier's ideas. It had an immediate impact in America and was more important in the forties than was Owen's arrival in the twenties as a stimulus to communitarian enthusiasms.

Despite their two very different personalities, the essential beliefs of Owen and Fourier were similar. Both thought that the huge cities growing around industrial areas were inimical to human happiness. The alternative for Owen was a small, self-contained community consisting of between 800 and 1200 people, for Fourier a phalanx to contain between 1620 and 1800 individuals. Fourier shared Owen's conviction that "character is universally formed *for* and not *by* the individual," and that within these carefully conceived communities man would naturally become a more perfect creature.[8] Owen revived a practice of the Italian Renaissance, another age of great optimism about human nature, in designing a large architectural model of what his ideal community should look like, a hollow square one thousand feet long housing an academy, a chapel, ballrooms, and living quarters, equipped with all the modern conveniences. While Owen embraced technology, many of the communities of the next thirty years rejected it. Of all the religious sects, only the Oneida community encouraged the use of technology. Several utopian satires of the late nineteenth century, such as William Morris' *News from Nowhere* and W. D. Howells' *Through the Eye of the Needle,* criticized these groups for precisely this refusal to incorporate any of the facts of modernity into their communities.

Writing to Emerson in 1840, George Ripley explained that the purpose of Brook Farm was

> to insure a more natural union between intellectual and manual labor than now exists; to combine the thinker and the worker as far as possible, in the same individual; to guarantee the highest mental freedom, by providing all with labor adapted to their tastes and talents, and securing to them the fruits of their industry; to do away with the necessity of menial services by opening the benefits of education and the profits of labor to all; and thus to prepare a society of liberal, intelligent, and cultivated persons whose relations with each other would permit a more wholesome and simple life than can be led amidst the pressures of our competitive institutions.[9]

There could hardly be a more concise statement of the beliefs which Owen and Fourier shared with many other communitarians in the nineteenth century. While almost all of these communities involved some form of communism—modified by Fourier to the joint-stock principle—there was much more emphasis on psychological and moral values than on economic systems. Most agreed with Ripley about the dignity of work in every form and the desirability of combining the thinker and the worker in the same individual. Most shared Brook Farm's reflexive socialism: the belief in joint ownership and equal reward, in moderating earning and spending and working. All in order to "permit a more wholesome and simple life," to encourage the simple pleasures of personal relations.

The extravagant hopes and the disappointing reality of Owen's New Harmony community were fairly typical of the experiences of these groups in the decades between Owen's arrival in 1825 and the subsiding of the Fourierist enthusiasm in 1846. Arriving in America, Owen had for an audience such distinguished statesmen as Jefferson and Madison, President John Quincy Adams, several members of the Cabinet, the members of the Supreme Court, and the Congress. Finally, after one hundred triumphant days of discourses on the benefits of communitarian living, Owen was convinced that "the whole of this country is ready to commence a new empire upon the principle of public property and to discard private property and the uncharitable notion that man can form his own character as the foundation and root of all evil." [10] In the course of his public lectures, Owen had invited "the industrious and well disposed of all nations" to New Harmony, and within six weeks after its founding it had a population of eight hundred persons. Evidently a few of these people were something less than "industrious and well disposed." Owen's son described the population as a "heterogeneous collection of radicals, enthusiastic devotees to principle, honest latitudinarians and lazy theorists, with a sprinkling of unprincipled sharpers thrown in." [11] Everything considered, New Harmony had a better chance to succeed than did most of the other experiments which followed. Aside from Owen's galvanizing rhetoric, his abilities as a leader, and his financial backing, New Harmony had a ready-built village surrounded by twenty thousand acres of land which had been cultivated by the previous owners, the Rappites. But partly owing to Owen's periodic absences from the community as well as fundamental differences among the community members, serious problems arose within the first few months. Owen dealt with recurrent economic crises by continuing to pour more money into the venture. But there was very little that could be done about internal fissures other than to run through one constitution after another, a total of five in the first year. Within a few more months, the community had split into four discordant groups.

But the general enthusiasm about communitarian experiments was undampened by such disappointments. In the five years following the publication of Albert Brisbane's *Social Destiny of Man* in 1840, more than two dozen Fourierist phalanxes were started. During the same period, dozens of other communities were founded, ranging from the Brotherhood of the New Life, the first of a series of Spiritualist communities, to the Harmonial Vegetarian Society in Harmony Springs, Arkansas.

One of these experiments, the Oneida community, initiated a series of radical reforms, which, for all their originality, were still variations on the characteristic communitarian themes of the period. Like many of the other communal groups, the Perfectionists at Oneida gathered around the imposing figure of a strong leader. John Humphrey Noyes, the community's founder and leader for more than thirty years, combined an infectious idealism and practical intelligence. Under Noyes's leadership, the community had its root in Perfectionism, a radical Christian belief which taught that the Second

Coming of Christ happened in A.D. 70, and that in the period since then everything had been ready for the perfection of man. Thus by making one ingenious theological twist, the Perfectionists escaped from the brooding pessimism of the Puritan conception of man into sanguine hopefulness. While the Perfectionist belief was no guarantee of virtue, it raised the possibility that through personal exertion guided by the ideals of Christianity man could realize his own divinity. Each aspect of community life at Oneida was designed with this task in mind.

Noyes advocated a radical Christianity. As a young man in his mid-twenties, he renounced any allegiance to the United States government in a letter to William Lloyd Garrison:

> I have renounced active co-operation with the oppressor on whose territories I live; now I would find a way to put an end to his oppression. . . . I cannot attempt to reform him, because I am forbidden to cast pearls before swine. I must therefore either consent to remain a slave till God removes the tyrant, or I must commence war upon him, by a declaration of independence and other weapons suitable to the character of a son of God. . . . My hope of the millennium begins where Dr. Beecher's expires—at the overthrow of this nation.[12]

Like many other communities, the Perfectionists practiced a form of communism that reflected a social ideal more than an economic necessity. Their goal was to form a family of the whole, to dissolve the nuclear family in favor of a larger partnership held together by the same forces that bind people together in marriage. The Perfectionists abolished private ownership and substituted joint ownership of property and equal distribution of all goods. The most radical innovation that the community made was to extend this principle of communism to people as well as material goods. As a consequence, the

Perfectionists replaced conventional marriage with complex marriage.

Under this system of complex marriage, the community as a whole was the economic unit, and any man and woman in the group could freely cohabit after obtaining each other's consent through an intermediary. But there was a sharp distinction between the delights of casual or "amative" intercourse and the responsibilities of "propagative" intercourse. Always an intensely practical man, Noyes devoted an entire volume to the practice of male continence in "amative" intercourse. (Evidently the system worked very effectively. The records of the community show that only about a dozen accidental conceptions occurred during a period of more than two decades.) The participants in "propagative" intercourse were carefully chosen to produce children with superior spiritual and physical inheritances. Predictably, despite the Biblical authorities that Noyes cited in explaining group marriage, it, more than any of his other reforms, aroused the indignation of outsiders. The Perfectionists had come to Oneida after being chased out of Putney, Vermont. And even in Oneida, where they were generally respected for their industry and their craftsmanship, Noyes and his followers were periodically harassed for their radical beliefs.

Like the Fourierist and Owenite movements, the Oneida Community was populated by middle-class idealists. Many had been farmers; some had been professional people. Most of them were well educated. At least half the members were over forty-five. Noyes, like many of the others who took leading roles in the dissemination of communitarian ideas, was fairly young when the community started. But there was no point in the history of the community at which it consisted mainly of young people, like the communes of the counter culture a century later. One of the important reasons for the success

of the Oneida colony was the care that it took in select-
ing new members. Compared with New Harmony, which
began and apparently ended as a heterogeneous group of
strangers, at Oneida many of the members had been
acquainted before they formed together as a community.
Even when the membership grew to more than two
hundred, the Perfectionists maintained a sense of community that New Harmony never achieved.

One of the ways in which this sense of community was
sustained was through the practice of mutual criticism.
Oneida shared with most of the other communities a concern for self-improvement. For some groups, this became
a highly ritualized concern. The Ephrata colony required
each member to prepare a weekly statement of his spiritual condition. At Oneida, mutual criticism was used to
encourage spiritual growth, but it was also a disciplinary
technique as well as a primitive form of psychoanalysis.
In some respects, it anticipated the use of encounter
groups a century later. As Father Noyes described it:

> This system takes the place of backbiting in ordinary
> society, and is regarded as one of the greatest means
> of improvement and fellowship. All the members are
> accustomed to voluntarily invite the benefit of this
> ordinance from time to time. Sometimes persons are
> criticized by the entire family; at other times by a
> committee of six, eight, twelve or more, selected by
> themselves from among those best acquainted with
> them, and best able to do justice to their character.
> . . . It is an ordeal which reveals insincerity and selfish-
> ness; but it also often takes the form of commendation,
> and reveals hidden virtues as well as secret faults. It
> is always acceptable to those who wish to see them-
> selves as others see them.[13]

Very few of the nineteenth-century communes joined
idealism with economic success as the Perfectionists did.

Like most of the other groups, they first attempted to earn a living through farming. But farming is a notoriously difficult way to support a self-sufficient community, and Noyes later explained that the reason for the failure of so many of them was their "land mania," the unwillingness to turn to any other sort of industry. The Perfectionists came well endowed with the funds to experiment with a number of different enterprises. They started with a saw mill and a flour mill, turned to the manufacture of silk thread and traveling bags, and finally turned a profit with the manufacture of the Newhouse animal trap, a crude product for a spiritual community. Years later, the most visible remnant of this community which started in determined idealism was a highly solvent corporation, Oneida Ltd. Similarly, the name of the Amana community in Iowa is kept alive by a line of refrigerators. And the Shakers are best remembered for their practical innovations, the flathead broom which we still use and the split wooden clothespin.

Along with almost every other community of this period, New Harmony ended in discord. By the end of the century only a few anarchist and religious colonies remained. Judging from their longevity, most of them had been conspicuous failures. The average life-span of the Fourierist communes was one to two years. Of the non-religious communities, the North American Phalanx lasted longest, for almost thirteen years. The religious communities fared better, proving the truth of Nordhoff's assertion that "a commune, to exist harmoniously, must be composed of persons who are of one mind upon some question, which to them shall appear so important as to take the place of religion, if it is not essentially religious; though it need not be fanatically held." [14] The Oneida, Aurora, Bethel, and Zoarite communities—all religious groups—lasted more than twenty-five years. The Rappites, the Shakers, and the Ephrata colony lasted more than a hundred years.

Why did a movement that caused so much excitement and attracted so many followers end in such a dreary catalog of failures? Noyes concluded his history of the movement with the testimony of dozens of disillusioned leaders remembering petty quarrels over land titles, mismanagement, and economic failures. One of them gave up his communal experiment with "a conviction that the theory of Communism could not be carried out in practice; that the attempt was premature, the time had not yet arrived, and the necessary conditions did not yet exist." The Sylvania Association ended with the complaint that "Idle and greedy people find their way into such attempts and soon show forth their character by burdening others with too much labor, and in time of scarcity supplying themselves with more than their allowance of various necessities, instead of taking less." [15] After three years, Robert Owen pronounced his verdict on New Harmony: "The attempt to unite a number of strangers not previously educated for the purpose, who should live together as a common family, was premature." He concluded that "the habits of the individual system die hard." [16]

A. J. Macdonald, the self-appointed historian of the movement who had spent years traveling from one community to another, concluded that after "seeing harsh reality" he could no longer sustain his hopes about the future of socialism. He confessed that he "had imagined mankind better than they are." [17] And Horace Greeley expressed a sentiment which could well serve as the epitaph for the whole movement:

> A serious obstacle to the success of any socialistic experiment must always be confronted. I allude to the kind of persons who are naturally attracted to it. Along

with many noble and lofty souls, whose impulses are
purely philanthropic, and who are willing to labor and
suffer reproach for any cause that promises to benefit
mankind, there throng scores of whom the world is
quite worthy—the conceited, played-out, the idle, and
the good-for-nothing generally; who, finding themselves utterly out of place and at a discount in the
world as it is, rashly conclude that they are exactly
fitted for the world as it ought to be.[18]

The conditions that had been favorable to the formation of small communities had changed by the end of the
nineteenth century. The frontier was settled, and land
was no longer as readily available. The scale of things
had changed, too. In the 1820's, America was a nation of
small towns and small-scale industry, and the notion of
forming a self-sufficient community of several hundred
people was no anachronism. By the end of the century
the assumption of plasticity, that institutions and habits
were still being formed, was outmoded. The task for
social idealists was to deal with existing institutions rather
than to form new ones. But the most substantial change
during this period had little to do with specific social
or economic developments. During the 1800's, rightly
called the Century of Great Hope, Owen's belief in individual improvement through the formation of ideal communities was the indispensable cornerstone of the
communitarian movement. By the end of the century
there were still utopian novelists, but very few people
who believed that utopia was achievable.

Writing in 1965 about the communal experiments of
the nineteenth century, Maren Lockwood concluded that
"today, the utopian community is an anomaly, a curious
revival of a dead tradition." [19] In 1965, it made very good
sense to relegate communitarian experiments to the status
of a curious historical footnote. After all, how could
communitarianism be modulated into the key of the

twentieth century? And why should an idea which had languished for more than half a century be revived? Yet by 1968 there were more communal experiments in this country than had existed at any point in the nineteenth century. Where those communes were large groups cemented by strong leadership, today's communes are small and anarchistic. Where many of them were highly structured communities in which individual behavior was strictly regimented, the communities of today are consciously unstructured, the lives of their members purposefully unregulated. Where those groups consisted of men, women, and children of all ages, the communes of today consist mainly of young people in their late teens and early twenties. Yet, in a curiously unutopian sense, the communes of the counter culture are a revival of the nineteenth-century theme, attempts to effect radical change through small communitarian experiments.

3 : Beyond Politics

"Escape from this! Bestir Yourself! Move into the Wider Realm!"   —Faust

"Turn on, tune in, drop out."   —Timothy Leary

During the campus revolts several years ago, a cartoon showed two college administrators walking past a student-occupied university building. Long-haired students were hanging out of the windows, the North Vietnamese flag was flying, and there was a huge sign with the crudely lettered message: LIBERATED TERRITORY. One administrator turned to the other and said, "I think they're trying to tell us something."

Most people have long since realized that in the bewildering variety of the protest movement and the counter culture there is, indeed, a message. But what that message *is* isn't entirely clear. When the counter culture is out in full force, as it was during the antiwar demonstration at the Pentagon in 1967, the protesters ran the gamut from old-line Marxists to witches and warlocks who were on hand to exorcise the Pentagon. Maybe, as Theodore Roszak has suggested, it is more like a medieval crusade, a procession—constantly in flux—in which a dozen different causes are loosely united under a single banner.

On the same weekend when the Pentagon was besieged, the cofounders of Liberation News Service, Ray Mungo and Marshall Bloom, decided to call a meeting of its constituents in an abandoned loft in Washington. LNS's goal was to provide a single news service for campus editors, black militants, anarchists, Communists, astrology freaks, pacifists, the Mexican-American liberation fighters, and an assortment of other activist organizations and their respective journals. Predictably, the meeting was something less than a model of parliamentary procedure. The college editors were interested in campus revolution, the freaks in cultural revolution, the pacifists in war, and the anarchists in the dissolution of any organization, including LNS. After the ritual attempt to evict as many members of the establishment press as could be identified, the meeting progressed by digression. Walt Bowart of the *East Village Other*, wearing an Indian headdress, began a long poem about the underground. There were charges of embezzlement and thievery in the Underground Press Syndicate, followed by another poetry reading by Allen Cohen of the San Francisco *Oracle*, which precipitated a lengthy poetry competition between Indian forces of the *EVO* and the Hare Krishna heads from the *Oracle*. Meanwhile, several draft cards were burned, and a fistfight broke out among warring factions within the antiwar organization. All of this was punctuated (or perhaps summarized?) by someone who kept shouting at the LNS organizers: "Do your thing! Do your thing!" [1]

The problem is to make sense out of all these factions within the counter culture. The best way to begin is to look at the tensions between militant activists and hippies, at the differences between political radicals and the apolitical radicals who constitute the psychedelic Left. Militant activists are in the tradition of the Old Left, with a program of toppling the power structure through revolution and changing the society from the top down. The hippie is in the tradition of Beat bohemianism, attempting to forge an alternative life style, to change the society from the bottom up. This is the tension which Rick Margolies has called the "wheelie-feelie polarization." The "wheelies" are the politicos, concerned about the public task of changing institutions and power relationships. The "feelies" are the artists, the psychologists, and the shamans of the movement, concerned about the private tasks of expanding consciousness, of becoming more gentle, sensitive, and expressive.[2]

The differences between these two orientations are enormous. The activist tries to organize an effective revolutionary group, a task-oriented organization, to meet the stern demands of the revolutionary ethic. In the hip program of self-exploration, there is no agenda of work to be performed, no schedule of revolutionary activities. To quote Henry Miller's *Tropic of Capricorn,* "There is only one great adventure, and that is inward towards the self, and for that time nor space nor even deeds matter." As Paul Goodman has pointed out, this is very close to the religious dilemma of faith versus works.[3] For the hippie, all works, all attempts to act effectively, are corrupt. Only right consciousness can avail. The activist accuses the hippie of futile sentimentalism, of becoming preoccupied with personal needs and hang-ups, of allowing the growth of an inhuman power structure. The hippie replies that militants are on a "power trip," that their human relations are corrupted in the very act of revolution, that they are involved in a self-defeating pattern of escalating violence. On the one hand, confrontation politics, urban guerrillas, and talk of a "people's war." And on the other, exotic religion, psychedelic explorations, and communal quietism. Two very different and often contradictory strategies.

This is the reason for so much of the dissension within the counter culture. Many of the confrontations between activists and hippies leave one wondering whether they have anything in common. Despite the fact that the Black Panthers' magazine featured an article entitled "The Hippies Are Not Our Enemies," the counter culture often feels more like a shotgun marriage than a natural alliance. In a widely circulated issue of the San Francisco *Oracle* in 1967, Timothy Leary flatly denied that any reconciliation was possible: "I say that there is a great difference— I say a completely incompatible difference—between the leftist activist movement and the psychedelic religious movement." More recently, John Lennon and John Hoyland, a British radical, exchanged letters in the *Black Dwarf* about this split. Hoyland argued that the system is inhuman and must be destroyed before it destroys any more lives. Lennon answered by defending the lyrics of the Beatles' song, "Revolution":

> Well, you know
> we all want to change the world.
> But when you talk about destruction,
> Don't you know you can count me out.
>
> You say you'll change a constitution
> well, you know
> we all want to change your head.
> You tell me it's the institution,
> well, you know
> you better free your mind instead.

Hoyland had the final word, the familiar New Left answer to those who drop out of politics: "What makes you so sure that a lot of us haven't changed our heads in something like the way you recommend—and then found out it wasn't enough, because you simply cannot be turned on and happy when you know that kids are being roasted to death in Vietnam, when all around you, you see people's individualism being stunted by the system."

Yet for all the differences between radical activism and hip-Beat bohemianism, each of these perspectives has an important contribution to make to the other. Several New Left organizations, notably SDS and SNCC, recognized this as a creative tension. In one of the working papers for the June, 1965, SDS convention, Richard Flacks discussed the problems of a movement which combines personal and political goals:

> If I understand what we are trying to work on when we say we are building a "movement," I think it has to do with two types of goals. One, which we might call "existential humanism," is expressed by the desire to change the way we, as individuals, actually live and deal with other people. . . . Second, we say that we seek a radical transformation of the social order. In short, that we act politically because our values cannot be realized in any durable sense without a reconstruction of the political and social system.
>
> I think it is inescapable that our movement must encompass both sets of orientations. It is clear that a politics apart from an existential ethics becomes increasingly manipulative, power-oriented, sacrificial of human lives and soul—it is corrupted. The danger involved in a social movement that is apolitical . . . is that of irresponsibility: of a search for personally satisfying modes of life while abandoning the possibility of helping others to change theirs; of placing tremendous hope in the immediate community for achieving personal salvation and gratification—then realizing that these possibilities are, after all, limited, and consequently, suffering disillusionment.[4]

It was easy enough in the early sixties to distinguish activists and hippies, to distinguish political from personal goals. But many of the most significant developments in the counter culture during the last decade, such as the Yippie strategy, have resulted from a blending of styles. Both the rhetoric and the logic of radical activism have changed, and hippies and activists have converged under the banner of the cultural revolution. For part of this variegated crusade called the counter culture that began back in the dim, distant idealism of the civil-rights movement, the course of progressive disenchantment over the past decade led first beyond social reform, then beyond protest to resistance, and finally beyond politics to the communal strategy in the cultural revolution.

Everyone in the counter culture has his own history of the events of the last decade. For some people, the whole thing began in the late fifties with Allen Ginsberg's *Howl* and Jack Kerouac's *On the Road*. For others, it began with the Montgomery bus boycott or the organization of SNCC and SDS in 1960. What is important is not to construct a chronology of the movement in the futile hope of understanding its trajectory and predicting its course. It is rather the attempt to look at the events of the past few years to try to understand the present. Like Alice explaining to the caterpillar that "at least I know who I was when I got up this morning, but I think I must have changed several times since then," the whole movement has shifted its direction and its mood too often and too rapidly to understand itself.

It is convenient to sort out the events of the decade into three periods. The first phase, roughly from 1960 to 1964, was the idealistic civil-rights era. During the second phase, from 1964 to 1968, the radical critique was formulated and activist and hip styles started to converge. The third phase began in 1968 at the Chicago Democratic Convention, and includes the development of the Yippie strategy, official repression of many parts of the counter culture, and the rapid growth of the communal movement.

Someone once explained to me that the civil-rights movement began when students unexpectedly started to take their high-school civics texts seriously. While this is certainly not the whole truth, it's an intriguing attempt to understand why in the early sixties so many Americans started to think about unfinished business on the agenda of guaranteed rights. Two items on this list received special attention: racism and poverty. While the Supreme Court had recognized in 1954 that "separate but equal" schools were inherently unequal, no single event dramatized the fact that America was still a racist society as clearly as a sit-in by four black students in a F. W. Woolworth store in Greensboro, North Carolina, in 1960. And while it was obvious that not everyone in the affluent society had a split-level home in the suburbs, somehow poverty was first recognized as a national problem with the publication of Michael Harrington's *The Other America* in 1962. Within six weeks after the sit-in in Greensboro, there were protests throughout the South against the fact that Negroes were denied the use of white lunch counters and public toilets. A few months later, sit-ins had grown into a nation-wide interracial protest against racism, and on campuses across the country something called student activism had begun.

Whatever the tangible results of this early activist period, it was clearly the end of an era of comatose privatism, at least among large segments of the younger generation. In the fifties David Riesman had criticized America as a nation of "political consumers." The surveys agreed, drawing a portrait of a nation consumed by private ambitions and undistracted by political and social issues. One of these, a survey of American college youth conducted in 1957, concluded that a dominant characteristic of students in the current generation is that they are gloriously contented both in regard to their present day-to-day activity and their outlook for the future. . . . American students are likewise dutifully responsive toward government. They expect to obey its laws, pay its taxes, serve in its armed forces—without complaint, but without enthusiasm. They will discharge the obligations demanded of them though they will not voluntarily contribute to the public welfare. Nor do they particularly desire an influential voice in public policy. . . . They are politically irresponsible, and often politically illiterate as well.[5]

By the early sixties, many young people were not only aware of poverty, racism, and the problems abroad that attracted the attention of the Peace Corps, but they believed that all this unfinished business could be completed through vigorous reform. If this assumption seems unbearably naive a decade later, it is also an indication of how rapidly things have changed. SDS's 1962 Port Huron Statement emphasized "participatory democracy," the importance of extending decision-making to as many people as possible. The answer to the privatism of the fifties was apparently that the most critical national problems could be solved if only there was widespread political participation. This was the politics of an age of consensus: It was assumed that the major institutions were still sound, that they needed only minor readjustments. As late as 1965, Paul Booth stated that SDS was basically a reformist organization, that its purpose was "to build, not burn." In the activism of those first few years of the sixties, there was a whole new set of protest tactics, almost all of them nonviolent. And the official reaction was remarkably different from what it would be a few years later. The courts supported the right to protest, and thus encouraged the movement.

Things happened so quickly and changed so convulsively from 1964 to 1968 that it is difficult in retrospect to sort it all out. Four years after a landslide re-election in 1964, there was a virulent "Dump Johnson" movement, and the President who had been elected by the largest plurality in recent history was forced not to seek re-election. Between 1964 and 1968, campus recruitment for the Peace Corps, which was the clearest expression of Kennedy-era idealism, dropped by 40 percent. In response to Johnson's declaration of a "War on Poverty" and his commitment to "The Great Society," there were riots in Watts, then Detroit and a dozen other cities. In Detroit, which had boasted a reputation as a model city with no "black problem," the police force ordered Stoner machine guns, prisoner buses, and chemical Mace dispensers to encourage a little more law and order. Assassinations, mass murders, and daily death counts from Southeast Asia all denied the comfortable assumption that violence had very little to do with the American way of life. National crime statistics show that, starting in 1964, there was a rapid increase in the amount of violent crime. While the futility of liberal programs for the urban poor was demonstrated each "long, hot summer," liberals' "explanations" of Vietnam became more transparently false each time there was a new escalation of the fighting. The combined effect of the war, the Johnson Administration, the racial crises in the cities, and the failure of the universities to respond to students' demands for full citizenship was to kill all the hopefulness of the civil-rights era and to transform the protest movement into a radically disaffected insurgency.

Judging both from its stated purpose and its tactics, the Free Speech Movement at Berkeley in the last few months of 1964 was very closely related to the civil-rights protests in the South. The issue that provided its impetus—like the issue in the South—was the abridgment

of constitutionally guaranteed rights. If a university administration building was a new setting for a sit-in, the
tactic itself had been learned in civil-rights activities
from which Mario Savio, FSM's major spokesman, and
many others there had recently returned.

Yet by December the FSM had grown far beyond civil
rights and had sounded all the themes of the radical
activism that was to be characteristic of the later sixties.
Rather than focusing on any specific issue, the FSM
became a revolt against liberal bureaucracy. Rather than
simply demanding the right to due process and an end
to administrative edicts that suppressed student political
expression, the thrust of the Movement was an attack
against the university as an embodiment of hypocritical
liberalism. The University of California was solidly implicated in the failure of the society to live up to its
ideals: It worked closely with large corporations and its
scientists performed research for the military. While pro-
fessing a commitment to freedom and democracy, it
seemed to have accepted a role as handmaiden to the
government, the large corporations, and *their* definition
of national priorities. Starting in Berkeley, the university
became both the major base of the radical movement and
the target of many of its activities, including protests
against on-campus recruitment by defense industries and
ROTC training of military personnel. The university was
also a symbol of a way of life, a reflection of what was
most corrupt and bankrupt in American values and institutions. After several years of civil-rights activities, most
students had come to believe that racism and discrimination were not just temporary blemishes on the face of a
healthy society. Like the logic of corporate capitalism,
or the escalating war in Vietnam which increasingly
displaced civil rights as the major issue, racism and discrimination were the results of a system that was fundamentally cancerous. The movement which had begun in

the civil-rights era as an attempt to take seriously America's ratified values had shifted to a radical critique of the society's most basic features.

During the earlier fight against racism, the movement had been intensely idealistic. Many of those who fought hardest for an end to discrimination and who most wanted to change this society so that everyone would have an equal place in it were children of the middle class. It was hardly the case that these students became activists because they wanted a place for themselves; most of them did not personally benefit from civil-rights reforms at all. At Berkeley, the task was not to guarantee that everyone had an equal place in the society; it was the more difficult task of erecting a society in which one would want to have a place. And this was a very different kind of idealism. Propelled largely by middle-class youths, as it has been ever since, it became a revolt against a bourgeois society which had been quite successful in performing according to its own standards. With a profound disrespect for the aspirations and values of bourgeois culture, this new radicalism moved away from the earlier emphasis on the extension of rights and the equal distribution of goods. Rather than defining freedom in economic and political terms, it redefined it in psychological and cultural terms.

The Free Speech Movement sounded a new mood, too, a shift from protest to resistance, articulated best by Mario Savio in a dramatic speech delivered from the steps of the administration building. "There is a time when the operations of the machine become so odious, make you so sick at heart, that you can't take part, you can't even tacitly take part. And you've got to put your body on the gears and upon the wheels, upon the levers, upon all the apparatus, and you've got to make it stop." [6] During the civil-rights phase, the official reaction had been to support the right to protest. At Berkeley, the police were called out and eight hundred students were arrested.

One other characteristic of the FSM signaled the beginning of a new phase. It had not been planned by any organized political groups, but by a broad coalition that included not just old radicals and students fresh from civil-rights activities, but also many people from the San Francisco Bay Area hip bohemian community. If it was an easy task in the early sixties to distinguish activists and Beat-hip bohemians, by the mid-sixties they were likely to be demonstrating side by side. And the concern for a new life style, which in the fifties had been one of the main emphases of Beat culture, had attained a new status among activists.

Very quickly, although hardly in unison, the protest movement abandoned the liberal critique of the war as bad policy in favor of the radical critique of the war as a result of an imperialist structure. SNCC formulated the ghetto-equals-colony analysis. The theory of imperialism accounted for both the war and the ghettos, and as a consequence the black revolts in American cities were projected into an international framework. The common enemy was capitalism. If there was any question about whether the civil-rights era was over by 1965, SNCC introduced Black Power, which implied a fundamental shift from integrationism to separatist-nationalist politics. Soon after, SDS moved beyond reform and adopted a student-power strategy.

This increasingly militant resistance strategy was an attempt to move beyond any particular issue—whether racism, Vietnam, or university reform—and to bring about radical solidarity among all the elements within the movement. Since the radical critique implicated the whole society there was a profusion of issues, each of which demanded an equally passionate response. After the momentum of a particular issue was spent, the momentum

of the movement was still there, to be redirected toward
new issues. It was a battle in which there was no front
line but a series of skirmishes. There were the issues of
university liberation and ghetto poverty, grape boycotts,
and rallies on abortion, dope, women's rights, and a dozen
other issues. Increasingly, militants were rebels with too
many causes. Like Byron, torn between the desire to fight
in the Greek War of Independence or to join the turmoil
in South America, the activist's dilemma was to make a
choice among an assortment of issues.

Yet the whole radical movement was loosely joined
together by a sense of the enemy, the "Establishment,"
an oppressive conspiracy led by government and corporate leaders. As the issue was not piecemeal reform but
the reconstruction of the society, no single concession,
no new policy could anesthetize the movement. Thus it
came as no surprise when, in a CBS news special on "The
College Turmoil," the presidents of three major universities—Michigan, Brandeis, and San Francisco State—
agreed that if the war in Vietnam were to end immediately, it would do nothing to end the student revolt.

The hip bohemian community was rapidly changing
during this same period in the mid-sixties. Its predeces-
sors during the fifties and early sixties, the Beatniks, had
rejected the conformity and materialism of the middle
class and had begun excursions into drugs, sexual experimentation, poetry, and music. But because they represented a tiny rebellion and not a very visible threat to
the status quo, they enjoyed the luxury of remaining
apolitical and generally free from harassment. Soon after
being rechristened the "hippie" movement in the mid-
sixties, this new bohemianism was no longer hidden from
the publc eye or immune from official harassment. By
1967, because of the draft, drugs, and the visible threat
of such centers as Haight-Ashbury, there was another un-
declared but escalating war—this one against the hippies.

Most of the protest movement grew out of a highly idealistic concern for social issues, but one part of it— draft resistance, the widespread refusal to accept induction—sprang from self-interest. When the Selective Service Commission retaliated in 1965 against draft-card burners, that action radicalized many young people who were otherwise not very much interested in political issues, including many within the bohemian community. By 1967, the National Student Association estimated that 35,000 students on campuses across the country had participated in demonstrations against the war.

But a more immediate cause of official harassment was widespread drug usage. Although psychedelics had been used in the early sixties, the popular use of mescaline, LSD, and other hallucinogens didn't begin until 1965. In January, 1966, the first "head" shop opened in Haight-Ashbury, featuring hallucinogenic manuals and psychedelic hardware, and the Haight became a psychedelic community. The whole area between the panhandle of Golden Gate Park and the slope of Mount Sutro was covered with psychedelic posters and paisley-painted VW vans. Just as obviously psychedelic were the new folk-rock groups emerging in San Francisco such as the Grateful Dead and Jefferson Airplane. In more important if less obvious ways the life style of Haight-Ashbury was the noncompetitive, passive, communal psychedelic style. LSD and mescaline were the most important set-breakers, the most effective proselytizers for a new kind of consciousness and a new way of life. And, temporarily at least, Haight-Ashbury was the mecca of that new consciousness.

Later in 1966, LSD was declared illegal both in the United States and Britain, and Timothy Leary was arrested at his *ashram* at Millbrook, New York, for possession of marijuana. The new prohibition era had begun. As if Vietnam, escalating draft calls, urban riots, unresponsive universities, and the Johnson Administration weren't enough to deaden whatever idealism was left among students, the government labeled as criminals hundreds of thousands of young drug users, and obtusely admitted its own ignorance about drugs by enforcing severe laws against the possession of even the mildest ones, such as marijuana.

At first merely the symbolic center of the movement, by 1967 the Haight was inundated with new recruits from the hinterlands. First there was the Be-In in Golden Gate Park, a gathering of twenty thousand that demonstrated a collective strength that the Beats had never had. Then there was the Summer of Love, a product of media attention if there ever was one. Hippies were News. There were daily hippie headlines in the San Francisco *Chronicle* (which had invented the word "hippie" in the first place). And *Time* magazine conferred the distinction of "the vibrant epicenter of America's hippie movement" on Haight-Ashbury just a few months before its collapse.

One day a headline in the *Chronicle* that "100,000 WILL INVADE HAIGHT–ASHBURY THIS SUMMER." The next day the announcement that "MAYOR SHELLEY DECLARES WAR ON HAIGHT–ASHBURY." Hippies were officially declared *personae non gratae*. After a period of tacit cooperation, the city's public agencies withdrew their services and created a climate of confrontation. Meanwhile, the streets and stairwells of Haight-Ashbury became clotted, and then, like any overused artery, they ruptured. By the fall, there was the "Death of Hippie" ceremony and meetings on how to save the neighborhood. Only slightly more than a year later, there were no more Day-Glo-painted VW buses and no more tribal gatherings. The neighborhood had deteriorated beyond repair; the storefronts were covered with sheets of plywood and the streets with broken glass.

The Haight became a drug ghetto, a teenage slum. Its former residents had left for the North Beach area a few miles away, or gone across the Bay to Telegraph Avenue in Berkeley. And by 1968, the migration to rural communes in Sonoma and Mendocino counties north of the city began. Those who were serious about finding a place for the new culture realized that it was much too fragile to survive in the city. If there was any place left where people could get by with a little help from their friends, where they could escape reporters and harassment, it was the country.

Nineteen sixty-eight brought the first of a flurry of student strikes, the May Days in France, and the Democratic Convention. In Chicago, a new alternative was unveiled, which provided a middle ground between the hip communal style and an increasingly violent resistance strategy. Take equal parts of activist and hippie, marinate in McLuhan and Marx (not dowdy old Karl but the zany brothers of the same name), season with LSD, and what do you have? Youth International Party. "Yippee! Yippee! Say it loud and you'll see what we mean!" Even if the Yippies were really not a movement at all, but only a slogan created by three men—Abbie Hoffman, Jerry Rubin, and Paul Krassner—Yippie represented an alternative to the sober, self-conscious revolutionary style. It was a new model of political action which in its antiorganizational and antipower predispositions carried two characteristic New Left attitudes to an extreme. And it was a pro-acid, pro-play movement which insisted that the only way to run a revolution is to have fun while doing it.

The Yippies had no party organization, no membership lists, no predefined revolutionary tracts dictating What Is To Be Done. In their place they substituted revolution as media-freaking, revolution as improvisatory theater in which Rubin and Hoffman were the impresarios and the participants were encouraged to stage their own myths. After all, if the media had been partially responsible for the wilting of "flower power," why couldn't they be used to promote rather than destroy a new kind of revolution?

Rather than taking the traditional role of revolutionary vanguard, the Yippies introduced the "Festival of Life" in Chicago. The Festival was both agitation and play, at the same time a means and an end. The Situationists, one of the student groups that was influential in the May Days in France, had already formulated a very similar strategy. As their manifesto stated it:

> Proletarian revolutions will be festivals or they will not be, for the life they herald will itself be created in festivity. Play is the ultimate rationality of this festival, living without boredom and enjoying without limitation are the only rules that will be recognized.[7]

Having finished a practice round at the Pentagon a few months before, the Yippies were out in full swing at Chicago. While an assortment of radical groups were trying to figure out a plan of attack, the Yippies were mobilizing the hordes of young people prepared to pour into the city. The sensationally exaggerated advance publicity demonstrated the Yippie genius for media-exploitation: Even if nobody believed it, it created a mood and an expectation which became a self-fulfilling prophecy. The plans for the Festival of Life included a variety of edifying counter-Convention activities such as a nude grope-in for peace and prosperity, a joint-rolling contest, the election of Miss Yippie, and the presentation of the official Yippie candidate, Pigasus, fresh from New Mexico via Hugh Romney's Hog Farm Express.

The Yippies proposed politics without any formal organization, change without trying to grasp power. In *Revolution for the Hell of It,* a book that looks like ab-

solute nonsense from the point of view of the old politics, Abbie Hoffman warns that "People who take
themselves too seriously are power crazy. If they win, it
will be haircuts for all. Beware of power freaks." But
if, following the traditional top-down revolutionary party
formula, people run the risk of being corrupted in the
very act of revolution, what is the alternative? The Yippie response is simple: Don't fight the revolution on the
Establishment's terms. In an afterword to G. William
Domhoff's *How to Commit Revolution in Corporate
America,* Chester Anderson discusses this nonideological,
nonorganizational politics of play:

> It would appear that in the new society organization
> increases at function's expense, and that organization
> *per se* tends to perpetuate itself and increase in size
> like a galloping cancer until the original purpose of
> the organization withers away to a scrap of sentiment
> and a rag of tradition wholly without meaning or
> importance.
>
> Instead of the American Revolutionary Party, I pro-
> pose a casual association of revolutionary gangs, not
> bothering to co-ordinate or otherwise inhibit them,
> caring more to maintain good communications among
> them.
>
> Fuck leaders and uniforms and holy causes more im-
> portant than people. A gang that playfully corrupts
> the mayor's teenage son produces more important and
> enduring change than does the strictly disciplined,
> grim, and earnest assassination squad that gets his
> father . . . and if the opposition fails at first to recog-
> nize the revolutionary nature of our invention, that's
> the opposition's problem.

Whatever revolutionary strategy might be successful
in America today, the notion of storming the capital, of
any kind of violent revolution, is hopelessly antiquated.
While the state maintains a near-monopoly on the in-

struments of destruction, the only possibility lies in revolution from within. But the problem with the Yippie
model of revolution from within is that it is so difficult
to take it seriously as politics. In Abbie Hoffman's words,
"The peace movement has gone crazy and it's about
time." The result is a tactical catechism that bears not the
slightest resemblance to traditional radical politics:

QUESTION: How to harass imperturbable military police
          guarding the Pentagon?
ANSWER: Unzip their zippers.

QUESTION: How to undermine corporate capitalism?
ANSWER: Show your contempt by throwing money out on
          the floor of its shrine, the New York Stock
          Exchange.

QUESTION: How to deal with an impersonal federal
          marshal?
ANSWER: Squirt him with chemical LACE, a high-
          potency sex juice that will make him pull off his
          clothes and make love.

QUESTION: How to infiltrate the very highest levels of the
          military-industrial complex?
ANSWER: Attend one of Tricia Nixon's teas, and bring
          enough LSD for all the honored guests.

All in all, an attempt to redefine revolution, to toss
out the inherited terminology of the Old Left. An attempt to define the success of revolutionary activities in
terms of how much they affect people, not institutions.
In Chicago, the Yippies didn't oppose the Democrats
with an isolated political program; they posed an alternative way of life. They proposed that politics isn't
something that you do, it's something that you are. For
the Yippies politics and life style were inseparably
merged. A year later at that quintessential Yippie hap-

pening, the Conspiracy Trial, there they were all together: Hoffman and Rubin, Tom Hayden and Dave
Dellinger, along with Ginsberg, Leary, Arlo Guthrie, and
a cast of thousands. And what was on trial, for all the
world to see, was not the evanescent conspiracy charge,
but a way of life.

Chicago meant something else too—the surfacing of
the police state. There had been arrests of protesters
before 1968, but mainly the official reaction had been
a slap on the hand and a reprimand. In 1968, there were
the first of a series of conspiracy indictments (the Boston
Five and the Oakland Seven), open warfare on the Panthers, and the murder of three black students by state
troopers during a student rebellion at Orangeburg, South
Carolina. Not quite a decade after the sit-in of pacifist
blacks at a Greensboro, North Carolina, lunch counter,
the same town was the setting for an armed battle between students and the helicopters, nausea gas, and
the rifle power of the National Guard. Firmly committed
to nonviolence in the civil-rights era, the movement rapidly shifted to violent tactics both as self-defense and
psychic liberation. Before anyone understood very well
what the new vocabulary of insurgency and imperialism
meant, it became clear that it was at least a rhetorical
commitment to violence. For all the contradictions between the counter culture's concern for emotional ex-
pressiveness, for becoming more gentle and sensitive, and
its commitment to violence, black radicals and some white
radical groups, notably the Weathermen, became the self-
appointed demolition squad of the movement. And at
free universities across the country, the new course offerings included instruction in the use of small arms and
the construction of Molotov cocktails.

Nonviolence was accepted in 1960 by both blacks and
whites because it seemed to work. Within a few years,
the rhetoric of violence was a reaction to the apparent

impotence of nonviolent strategies as well as a response to the violence used by the government in suppressing the insurrection. Some concessions resulted from the demands of the early civil-rights workers, but the situation of most blacks remained unchanged. The first significant challenge to the nonviolence of Martin Luther King came from Malcolm X, who was followed by H. Rap Brown and the Black Panthers. Violence was useful as a tactic, Malcolm said, because America responded only to violence. He hoped that the threat of violence would be enough to force America to reform itself.

Malcolm introduced another idea that was to become important in the new ideology of violence: Violence is not only necessary as self-defense, it is also an essential act of self-assertion. Thus from tactical violence to violence as therapy. If so many of the events of the past few years reflect a cult of violence, a highly romanticized belief in the usefulness of a well-placed stick of dynamite, much of it has resulted from this ideological shift to expressive violence.

In one of the most popular books among radical activists in the last few years, *The Wretched of the Earth*, Frantz Fanon gives this idea its fullest expression. He understood violence as a spiritual act in which the colonized peoples were born as free men in the act of striking back at the colonial state. In the foreword to the book, Jean-Paul Sartre adds his words of approval: "Irrepressible violence . . . is man recreating himself." It is through "mad fury" that the wretched of the earth can "become men."

While this may be valid among the oppressed people of the African colonies where Fanon lived and worked as a psychiatrist, expressive violence as self-liberation rapidly degenerates into rhetorical nonsense among white radicals in this country. There would be a great deal to say for violence if it were an effective midwife in achiev-

ing a better society. But it is not only futile but dangerously inappropriate if it is the last resort of hatred, if
it is done only for expressive purposes with no hope of
any effect except enraged reaction. In their demolition
tactics, the advocates of violence within the counter
culture raise the bleak specter of revolution at any cost.
Like the very young Russian radical, Tkachev, who
wanted to liquidate everyone in Russia over twenty-five
years of age in order to usher in a new era, in their
limitless fervor these violent factions commit the mistake
that the New Left avoided: They subordinate people to
doctrine.

Despite the fact that a bomb explosion in General
Motors' Manhattan headquarters might exhilarate many
of those whose participation in the counter culture is
limited to a moratorium-day rally, the size of this demolition squad is minuscule. Since the Manhattan townhouse
explosion in which three members of the group were
killed, the Weathermen have apparently reconsidered
their original belief that the only useful revolutionary
acts are committed with bombs and guns.

At the beginning of the sixties, there had been two
easily distinguishable styles, the hippie and the activist.
By the late sixties, life style had become an important
issue in the cultural revolution. Hippies had been radicalized by busts, official harassment, and the Selective
Service Commission. In the Chicago Conspiracy Trial,
along with the defendants charged with political sub-
version, there was Allen Ginsberg, Om'ing and talking
about love, spirituality, and sexuality. In Berkeley, activists and hippies now digest political pamphlets and
psychedelic newspapers with no queasiness about fundamentally different styles of dissent. Several years after
announcing that there was a "completely incompatible
difference" between leftist activists and the psychedelic
religious movement, after having turned on, tuned in,

and dropped out—and having been arrested for his efforts—Timothy Leary was sprung from his prison cell
at San Luis Obispo with the help of the Weathermen.
And the Weathermen, for their part, have begun talking
about collectives. Which is to say that, despite the differences among the factions in the counter culture, we
can no longer make any neat distinctions between fundamentally different revolutionary agendas.

Perhaps the best way to understand the tactical alternatives which are available now in the counter culture
is to think of them as a spectrum of choices. At one
end are the recognizably political revolutionaries con-
centrating on the capturing of political power and re-
viving the Marxist-Leninist categories of class conflict
and anti-imperialism. At the other end of the spectrum
is the apolitical strategy, Rudi Dutschke's "long march
through all the institutions of the society," and an emphasis on dropping out of the mainstream society in
order to experiment with alternative life styles. There is
still the same split between a top-down "instant revolution" and a bottom-up revolution of life style which was
characteristic of the differences between activists and
hippies several years ago. But now there is a coherent
list of concerns shared by the whole counter culture. For
most people who have chosen the communal alternative
the priorities are: (1) expanding consciousness; (2) the
immediate physical environment; (3) other people; and
(4) power allocation and rearranging institutions. Political revolutionaries at the other end of the spectrum recognize the same four concerns, but would reverse the
priorities.

Holding all the factions together is the specter of the
apocalypse.[8] As George Wald commented, this is "a generation which is no longer sure that it has a future."
The first declaration of the Underground Press Syndicate in 1967 expressed a foreboding of imminent col-

lapse which would have been incomprehensible in the early sixties. The goals stated in that declaration were:

1. To warn the "civilized world" of its impending collapse.
2. To advise intelligently to prevent rapid collapse and make transition possible.
3. To fight a holding action in the dying cities.
4. To prepare the American people for the wilderness.
5. To offer as many alternatives to current problems as the mind can bear.

It is a generation that is acutely aware of that other threat, too, that we may be rushing toward 1984 and becoming a nation of anesthetized robots numbly moving from sterile suburbia to corporate work bins, more efficiently programmed than any of Orwell's proles. If this culture no longer has a future and radicalism is the only response, then the question is which strategy from this spectrum of tactical alternatives promises the best return.

While there is considerable evidence that student radicals aren't seduced into conservatism as soon as they leave the campus, the problem of finding viable channels for radical action is critical. Five years after the sit-in at Sproul Hall during the Free Speech Movement at Berkeley, two Detroit *Free Press* reporters surveyed the students who had been arrested there.[9] Their purpose was to find out how the radicalism of the rank-and-file members of that pioneer student revolt held up. In 1965, soon after the FSM ended, Hal Draper, a Socialist writer and a supporter of the Berkeley rebels, made a prediction that reflected the ardent hope of most of the older generation. He predicted that within ten years, "most of [the rebels] will be rising in the world and income, living in the suburbs, raising two or three babies, voting Democratic and wondering what on earth they were

doing in Sproul Hall—trying to remember and failing."
We are more than halfway through that ten-year period,
and Draper's prediction has yet to come true.

After five years of tumultuous social and political
change—as well as marriage, children, graduate school,
and careers—the group as a whole was as radical when
it was surveyed in 1969 as it had been during the Movement. But while the radical sympathies of the 230 students who completed questionnaires for the *Free Press*
survey had changed hardly at all, radical activity had
diminished. They were now graduate students, teachers,
or social workers, temporarily engaged in odd jobs, or
living in the suburbs as full-time mothers. Even though
many of them were no longer active in politics, most
shared the sentiments of one young man, now working
as a warehouseman in a hospital. "FSM influenced me
from then on out. Since then, I really can't take a job
in the Establishment without feeling that I'm copping
out. I'm inclined to, because I like comfort, but I really
can't do it." Rather than "rising in the world and income," as Draper predicted, the rebels are relatively
poor. Their average yearly income is between $2,500
and $5,000.

Ninety percent of the group supported the campus dis-
ruptions that followed the Berkeley example, even though
many of those demonstrations involved tactics which
were more violent and issues which were less clear than
those in the FSM. At the same time, though, more than
a third of them now felt that the Sproul Hall sit-in was
ineffective, and many of them were convinced of the
futility of any political activity. One girl spoke for the
minority of the rebels who said that the experience had
turned them away from politics and activism completely
and toward a private quest for fulfillment. "I think people have to go inward rather than outward," she said.

"I'm busy living the right life myself first, and I feel that I have to change myself."

In a study of the Berkeley drug colony in 1967, James T. Carey found that the hard-core acidheads there had completely rejected the possibility of changing the social order through political action. They had developed "a distinctive life style which celebrates political disengagement." [10] This comes as no surprise: It is the familiar difference between activist and hippie. But Carey also found that many of the heads were former activists who had decided that society was impervious to change. For them, it was a progression from radical activism to nonpolitical forms of rebellion. This same progression can be seen among many of the people who have chosen to live communally. Many of them are disenchanted activists or frustrated pacifists, people who distrust somber revolutionaries almost as much as straight society. They sense very keenly the frequently pathological mainspring of those who seek political power. One of them, a twenty-two-year-old who was initiated in a campus demonstration several years ago in which he was knocked down and arrested, is now living communally in the Taos, New Mexico, area. He completely rejects the program of the political revolutionaries: "Put them in power and they'd be on a power trip, putting their thing on me—and it'd be no different than it is now."

Most of the communal young have rejected the assumption that political revolution is going to usher in a new cultural order. The ritual response of an orthodox Marxist to anyone who asks how he could hope to change society without first changing as a person, changing his relations with others, and changing organizational structures is that all these things will happen . . . "after the revolution." Yet in the aftermath of every revolution in recent history the recurrent cry has been breach of promise. If there is one lesson to be drawn from this experience, it is that the revolutionary process cannot be separated from the revolutionary goal. The communal strategy is a reaction against a theory of revolution that deals in political and economic categories that bear no relationship to everyday life. The only goal of revolution is the liberation of daily life—and it cannot be justfied by appeals to universal categories of historical dialectics.

In periods of confidence about the possibilities of social reform, radical energies are applied at the political fulcrum. But a decade after the optimism of the civil-rights era, the mood is now one of despair about being unable to change society. It is a feeling of powerlessness in all but the most personal spheres of one's life. And both the resort to violence and the privatism of the communal style are expressions of this despair.

In two books that appeared in the mid-sixties, *Young Radicals* and *The Uncommitted,* Kenneth Keniston made a distinction between two styles of dissent. This distinction reflected, to some extent, the tenor of the mid-sixties, when there was much more hopefulness about the possibility of transforming the society. On the one hand, he discussed "alienated" students whose values were apolitical and aesthetic. These rebels were responsive to "romantic" themes of social criticism, the dehumanizing of society, its failure to provide "spiritual fulfillment," and its lack of aesthetic quality. The "uncommitted" care very little about appeals for social, economic, and political justice. Keniston compared these "alienated" students to young activists, who were "politically involved, humanitarian, and universalistic in values."

Which of these two types is now attracted to communal living? Neither, and both. To be sure, the communes do attract many of those who correspond to Keniston's "uncommitted," confused young people looking for some sort of sanctuary, for a moratorium from the heavy schedule of obligations waiting for them back in the mainstream society. In the late fifties, a study of the San Francisco Beat colony conducted by the psychiatrist Dr. Francis Rigney found that 60 percent "were so psychotic or crippled by tensions, anxiety, and neurosis as to be non-functional in the competitive world." [11] In the communes, there is a minority of these psychological casualties. Compared to this relatively small group, and those who are temporarily disengaged from the mainstream—the Clark Kent hippies and teenyboppers out for a fling—rural communes have attracted a large number of people who correspond to Keniston's "young radicals." These are people who would have been, and in some cases actually were, politically active in a period of greater optimism about the prospects of social reform.

What happened is that students who entered protest activities with the hope of changing institutions and power relationships left with a feeling of frustration, but also with an intangible sense of comradeship and the joys of togetherness. The university, which came billed as an "academic community," turned out to be just another impersonal bureaucracy; while student sit-ins, which promised at first only limited tactical advantages, delivered the elixir of community. As a Columbia professor described the climate in the four student-occupied buildings in spring, 1967, "an intense communal life emerged, in which students at last enjoyed a shared commitment and purpose." One of the major attractions of *any* movement, like the perverse attraction of war, is that it serves to unite a group of people in a common cause and a single faith. One of the major problems of any movement is to sustain this intoxicating atmosphere of shared purpose. It was this sense of community that turned out to be one of the most important by-products of the protest activities of the mid-sixties. Radically disaffected from the mainstream culture, these young people have reached a point at which life style itself is the only remaining form of protest. For them, the lesson of the sixties is the futility of political reform, and the only viable radical alternative is to begin to create a new society in microcosm, to plant the germ cells of a new social organism.

If there is such a thing as a manifesto for this communal strategy, it would have to be Ray Mungo's *Famous Long Ago*, a brightly written statement of the case for dropping out of politics.[12] Now a wizened old man in his mid-twenties, Mungo has the distinction of having participated in nearly every phase of the movement during the last decade. In his early stages, he progressed from "violent Marxism" to pacifism, and in the process was introduced to dope just a little earlier than most. In 1964, he discovered the war in Vietnam. In Mungo's words, "from Vietnam, I learned to despise my countrymen, my government, and the entire English-speaking world, with its history of genocide and international conquest. I was a normal kid."

If he was famous at all, it was in Boston where he was editor of the Boston University *News* in 1966–67, which specialized in items on draft resistance, the war, abortion reform, dope, and academic revolutions, and which had its moment of glory with an "Impeach Johnson" editorial which became a city-wide scandal. At graduation, he had a choice between graduate school and moving to Washington to help in the program of overthrowing the state as a cofounder of Liberation News Service. Naturally, he chose the latter. "Overthrowing the state seemed to me an excellent idea, it desperately needed to get done, and since if you want something done you must do it yourself, I said OK why not?"

Located on the forefront of what was happening in Washington, "the seat of evil in the world," Mungo put in his time manning the mimeos and mobilizing millions of students through the network of LNS-affiliated papers throughout the country. And then, in 1968, he was one of the first radical student leaders to drop out, a story which is best told in his own words:

> We were living in the heartland of death and failure, incapable of either reforming the decaying establishment or dealing it the final blow. . . . What we called the movement which started out as a peace-living opposition to slavery, racism, and war, has become an enslaving, racist, civil war of its own; in short, it died. Many of the people still active in the new movement are in reality dead men, killed off by bitterness and frustration and the unceasing attention of your television cameras. But many others have made the transition from the dying thing into a new living alternative which is trying again to save the world—save the planet, in fact. . . . Here's a lesson I honestly believe I learned in my lifetime: ideals cannot be institutionalized. You cannot put your ideals into practice, so to speak, in any way more "ambitious" than through your own private life.

After several years of the frustrations of powerlessness and the privations of city life, while all the time the goals of peace, justice, and freedom seemed to be receding into the distance, Mungo and his friends had their vision: "The word Vermont popped into our heads almost simultaneously. Vermont! Don't you see, a farm in Vermont! A free agrarian communal nineteenth-century wide-open healthy clean farm in green lofty mountains! A place to get together again, free of the poisonous vibrations of Washington and the useless gadgetry of urban stinking boogerin' America." This was the beginning of their "total moratorium on constructive participation in this society." In no time at all, Mungo and nine of his friends were at Montague Farm, reading Thoreau rather than news dispatches and putting university-trained hands to work chopping wood, weeding potatoes, and hauling maple-sugar sap.

"So much of the process of becoming free in my country, it seems," writes Mungo in his recent report entitled *Total Loss Farm*, "is in withdrawing from all the awful things we've been deliberately and systematically taught to need . . . so that a good deal of our manner and program must be negative rather than positive. We are the people who *do not do* all those corrupt things, etc. etc. But the positive, new and forward aspects of the life are coming on strong now. . . ."

The long road that began with sit-ins and then proceeded through war protests, university rebellions, and dreams of a new age born of violent insurrection led Ray Mungo and a few friends beyond politics to the rural isolation of Montague Farm. Having allowed Mungo to speak for himself so far, I should allow him to finish. "Let us now then cease with our complaining about the state the world is in, and make it *better*. We're not trying to convince the world—the world has an energy of its own, and we're only a tiny part of that. We're only trying to change ourselves, what a preoccupation! But if we get better, if I get better, that's tangible change, isn't it?"

4 : The Middle-Class Revolt

> We have begun to pose to ourselves the terrifying
> question: can it be true that our civilization is not
> *the* civilization?
>
> —Jacques Soustelle

We still practice the ancient ritual of killing the bearers
of bad news. Only the methods have changed. Occasionally the bearer is spared by conveniently denying the
fact that his message *is* bad news. But one way or
another, the effect is the same.

Take, for example, the reaction to disaffected young
radicals. Their critics haul out the heavy artillery of
psychological explanations: In order not to take the radicals' message seriously, it's useful to convince yourself
that they are less than sane, or that radicalism is nothing
more than the result of parental indulgence. Or the
critics use the peculiarly modern bludgeon of overexposure. "The way Americans deal with anything that
seems unmanageable," said Margaret Mead, "is to run it
into the ground by overuse. . . . We exaggerate, we
caricature, we overemphasize, and then we eliminate." [1]

Or the "generation gap" is dragged out to explain
youthful radicalism. Rather than explaining, it obfuscates.
I suspect that the generation gap has become a ritual

stop in nearly every discussion of the "youth problem," despite the accumulated evidence to the contrary, largely because it's such a neat way of dismissing what is unique about this generation's radicalism. After all, in the last fifty years, we've had the "lost generation," the jazz generation, the apathetic generation, and the Beat generation. This new radicalism can be dismissed as nothing more than a new wrinkle in the expected conflict between one generation and the next. The soothing message of the generation-gap explanation is that the problem is one of communication between the young and the old. It suggests that the differences are "merely generational," that a person's age determines his way of looking at things. With condescending smugness the conclusion is that young people will "know better when they grow up."

All of which are useful ways of dismissing the young radicals and denying the fact that they bring a very disturbing message. The conspicuous youths who grew up in the fifties were, with few exceptions, like their not-so-visible peers, but more successful. They were mainly interested in living the lives of their parents, only more so. Parents of the Depression era wanted economic security, their sons wanted affluence. Upward mobility was something more than a new phrase out of the sociological jargon. If the third-generation Jew was the most conspicuous participant in the American tropism from small-scale merchant to entrepreneur to lawyer or doctor or public servant, this was also the pattern of the whole. The difference that became palpably obvious several years ago was that a highly visible part of this new generation began to experiment with a life style radically different from that of their parents.

Yet despite the fact that while traveling on Route One from San Francisco to Big Sur it looks as though the whole generation has defected and joined a children's crusade, what was true in the fifties is still true. Despite the generation gap and media fascination with young radicals, most young people still subscribe to their parents' values with hardly a second thought. For example, one study conducted during the winter following the flurry of student activism in 1968 surveyed male seniors in colleges throughout the country. Its finding was that the middle-of-the-road youths now in college will provide a conservative ballast almost as secure as the present one. Only 24 percent of the seniors had ever used marijuana. Two-thirds reported that they agreed with their parents on most things. For three-quarters of them, the American system of higher education was "basically sound," and only 4 percent gave their unqualified support to SDS.[2] In other words, encouraging news to the majority of Americans who chose Richard Nixon, Billy Graham, Spiro Agnew, and Lyndon Johnson as the four "most admired" men in a 1969 Gallup Poll.

But to dismiss the message of radical youths because they are only a small minority of the younger generation is as foolish as the assumption that to be young is to be radical. What has been happening during the past few years makes much more sense if it is understood as a social-class phenomenon than as generational revolt. Understood as a defection of the children of the middle class, youthful radicalism takes on a very different kind of meaning.

Any revolt of the disadvantaged, such as the early civil-rights protests, is business as usual. It is a justifiable assertion of the rights of justice and an equal share in prosperity. For all the temporary discomforts and dislocations it causes, it is a way of shoring up the traditional verities, of taking the ratified values seriously, and pointing out that they haven't yet been delivered.

But the counter culture, and particularly the rural communal part of it, is a rebellion that consists mainly of recruits born in socially advantaged families. For these youths who were raised in affluent homes, the old revolutionary demands for greater access to institutions and the extension of democratic rights make no sense precisely because they will draw more people into a bourgeois society whose hollowness they have already experienced. "Middle-class living rooms are funeral parlors, and only undertakers will stay in them," as Peter Berg, a typically disaffected product of the middle class, was quoted as saying in *Newsweek*. "The United States standard of living is a bourgeois baby blanket for executives who scream in their sleep. Industrialization means sweat and insanity. Our fight is with job-wardens who would kill us through dumb work, insane wars, and a dumb money morality."

In a nonideological movement, perhaps the graffiti of the Paris revolution in 1968 was, in its own haphazard way, one of the best reflections of radical sentiments: "I take my desires to be reality because I believe in the reality of my desires." "Never work." "The more you consume, the less you live." "The boss needs you, you don't need him." "One does not buy happiness, one steals it." Or that masterpiece of graffiti from the May Days: "It is forbidden to forbid." The values of consumption, of deferring gratification, of work and productivity, in fact almost every one of the major assumptions and the most important symbolic rewards which have propelled American civilization, along with most of the Western world, are being called into question.

If material abundance and the achievement of a more or less equitable society were the measure of man, most Americans might heed Rousseau's derisive advice to the citizens of Geneva: "Your happiness is complete, and you have nothing to do but enjoy it; you require nothing more to be made perfectly happy than to know how to be satisfied with being so." [3] In the somnambulant fifties, it was particularly seductive to assume that prosperity would dissolve most problems. By the end of the sixties, a decade of the fastest economic growth this nation has ever known, it had become all too clear that prosperity leaves in its wake new problems, and harder ones.

Paradoxically, affluence generates both discontent and rebellion. Perhaps the most puzzling fact that emerged in the sixties was that white radicals came from the most economically, educationally, and socially privileged families. Studies of the family backgrounds of student radicals have been almost unanimous on this point. These students most frequently come from high-income families in which the parents are politically liberal. Almost all of the early campus protests happened at prestigious universities characterized by high aptitude scores and a large percentage of intellectually motivated students planning to complete college and graduate schools. Young radicals are frequently above-average students interested in the social sciences and the humanities. Because of the status of their families as well as their own scholastic performance they are in a position to enter the most desirable careers and to gain the most highly valued rewards that this society has to offer.

Since the first studies of student radicals in the mid-sixties, a number of factors such as peer influence and the increasing importance of issues which affect the immediate self-interest of students have combined to modify this portrait of the young radical. Radicalism is now accepted among a broad spectrum of students. The protests that began in such elite universities as Berkeley, Columbia, Michigan, Wisconsin, and Stanford have spread to non-elite colleges. At least one recent study, of the family backgrounds of SDS members at the University of Oregon, has found that the new radicals do not necessarily come from unusually privileged backgrounds.[4] But a substantial part of the counter culture still comes from the most advantaged stratum in this society.

One of the facts that the generation-gap idea hides is that there are more differences within the younger generation than between the young and the old. A higher proportion of young voters than older voters, for example, favored Wallace in the 1968 presidential election. This pattern was consistent both in and outside the southern states and was true regardless of whether the voters were grade school, high school, or college graduates.[5]

More importantly, the generation-gap idea denies the most interesting aspect of this rebellion, the continuity between parents' values and the beliefs and actions of their children. Like the families of the later protesters, the parents of most of those who were arrested in the Free Speech Movement at Berkeley were affluent and well educated. Their median income was about $16,000, and most of them had at least a bachelor's degree. Significantly, a majority of the parents of the students who were arrested there approved of the FSM. Many of the demonstrators' parents had been active in leftist politics in the thirties and forties. Despite the fact that very few of the parents are now politically active, as a group they are unusually interested in politics. Thirty percent of the protesters considered their parents to be as radical as they were.[6]

In his study of student radicals, Kenneth Keniston reached the same conclusion. He found that the great majority of radicals' parents applauded, approved, or at least accepted their activities. The significant generational difference appeared to be about the extent of their son's or daughter's radical commitment; parents' reservations were most often based on "practical" considerations, not value differences.[7]

Richard Flacks, who has made a number of important

contributions to an understanding of young radicals, has pointed out that the typical radical comes from a special type of family that is both upper-middle class and deeply committed to humanistic concerns for individual development, self-expression, and the social condition of others. "Activists are more 'radical' than their parents; but activists' parents are decidedly more liberal than others of their status. . . . The great majority of these students are attempting to fulfill and renew the political traditions of their families. . . . Activism is related to a complex of values, not ostensibly political, shared by both the students and their parents." [8] Both are disaffected from the political system and reject the competitive, status-oriented individualism of bourgeois culture.

The difference between the generations is that radicals are much more likely to *act* on their principles than their parents were. Raised in families in which affluence is taken for granted and humanistic values are shared, they have been urged to attend college, which in turn reinforces those values. Education is highly valued, not so much as a steppingstone to better jobs and higher income than their parents have had, but as a goal that is intrinsically worthwhile. Raised in homes that encourage individuality and autonomy, they have learned to be contemptuous of authority. Rather than following conventional career lines, they turn their attention to social conditions, a preoccupation that their affluent parents have encouraged by allowing them economic freedom, at least for a while. Earlier generations had extraordinary expectations of material wealth and occupational mobility. For this group of young people raised in affluent families the attention has shifted to the possibilities of immediate experience and the promise of personal fulfillment, as well as to an acute awareness of the existing institutional arrangements which contradict humanistic beliefs. The result is a rejection of the existing society and the search, whether political or apolitical, for alternatives.

This revolt of the children of the middle class is nothing new. To take just one example, at its height in 1902, most of the leaders of the Russian student movement were sons of doctors, teachers, and other professionals.[9] This is the same occupational group which is currently producing the greatest number of young radicals. But a middle-class revolt means something very different in America in the 1970's from what it meant in Russia at the turn of the century. No small part of the population, the middle class in America is already the overwhelmingly predominant class and promises to be more so. And it is the highly educated professional and technical sectors that are the most rapidly growing occupational groups. More and more families are hoping to send their children to college, where they will almost inevitably be influenced by, if not converted to, humanistic values and an anti-bourgeois, anticapitalistic ethic in the process of doing what they came for, getting an education in order to get better jobs in order to participate more fully in bourgeois capitalistic society. In short, this minority of radically disaffected young people from affluent middle-class homes may well be a prophetic minority.

To borrow a line from one of Warner Bros.' recent spectacles (which sounds like Rousseau's message to the citizens of Geneva modulated into the prevailing key of the twentieth century): "THX 1138: You are programmed for happiness. Why are you trying to escape? . . ."

The scene is a familiar one. On the bulletin board of the precinct station in the East Village there are pictures —hundreds of them—of standard-issue, freshly scrubbed teenagers, now runaways. And there are notes left by anxious parents:

Jonathan, age 16, long blond hair, last seen wearing bell bottoms and a work shirt marked with peace insignia, believed to be in the East Village or Vermont-area communes. $100 reward offered for information of whereabouts. Contact Mr. and Mrs. Robert Miller, Westport, Connecticut.

In 1967, after Linda Fitzpatrick, an eighteen-year-old suburban girl, was found murdered on a boiler-room floor on the Lower East Side, *Newsweek* reported that "almost overnight, the East Village seemed aswarm with parents searching for some of the 9,000 runaway children believed to be living the hippie life in New York." In other times, they would have run away to sea, or followed a traveling carnival, or joined a gypsy band. But they have no skills, it is no longer possible to run away to sea, and the boys face the draft.

To announce that this rebellion is idealistic is to commit the all-too-truism. Even the report of the Scranton Commission, predestined to the status of an "official" statement on the counter culture despite being denounced upon its birth by President Nixon, declared that "most of its members have high ideals. . . . They stress the need for humanity, equality, and the sacredness of life," while their parents are so "entrapped by materialism and competition" that they have lost their "sense of moral purpose." Unlike Marx's revolution, this is moral rebellion. Of course the demands of young radicals of all varieties are "nonnegotiable." Where a matter of principle is concerned, any compromise is capitulation.

In her book *On Violence*, Hannah Arendt comments, "if we inquire historically into the causes likely to transform *engagés* into *enragés*, it is not injustice that ranks first, but hypocrisy." [10] In the same way that Daumier looked at the fat, complacent middle class of nineteenth-century France, the purpose of much of the counter culture is to tear away the mask of middle-class hypocrisy, to expose its hollowness. The mood of most of the older generation suggests no need whatsoever to create a different and a better world. Even when the tactics of the young are stupid and self-defeating, the motivations of this rebellion are the right ones. If, as Michael Harrington remarked, "they drive you crazy with their morality," they are morally justified, reacting against the pathological passivity of most of the older generation.

This is one of the meanings of the slogan, often repeated and seldom followed, "You can't trust anyone over thirty." The suspicion is that only the young can keep their idealism intact. In many respects, youths are delegated the task of bearing the society's social and cultural values. In the same way and for the same reason that the Catholic Church denies family life to its priests, youth is well suited to the task of the "moral organ" of the society because it is, so to speak, between acts. The young are relatively unattached to family, particular communities, and careers. Their major commitment is to educational institutions, which emphasize the ideal aspects of the culture and require relatively few moral compromises. While the grown-ups, who are occupied with the business of running the bureaucracies of the world, are inevitably involved in compromises, preoccupied with tactics and the art of the practical, too much involved in the status quo to be able to afford to step aside and question its assumptions.[11]

It is those assumptions that the young are attacking. The most crucial aspect of youth's perception that middle-class society is morally hypocritical lies in its belief that the production ethic of industry and frugality is now irrelevant and therefore morally illegitimate. Like the space program which lost its early heroism and its short-lived attraction as the nation's leading spectator sport because it was too successful, the production ethic has been rendered obsolete through success. Material scarcity is no longer the most pressing problem, and therefore neither habits of industry nor the accumulation of wealth are any longer among the high virtues. "The fact that all the world goes after money," as Edward Bellamy once observed, "saves a man the necessity of anxiously debating what his life is for." For the young who have rejected the assumption of scarcity and the foregone conclusion that one's major business in life is to make money, the huge task is to find a way of life that is consistent with their values.

Their elders, so strongly influenced by the Depression and the war which followed, were concerned to an extraordinary extent with success and security. Probably more energetically than any previous generation, they pursued the goal of a worldly paradise based on material consumption. This version of the American Dream is embodied in the characteristic social setting of the postwar generation: suburbia. Although it was no new phenomenon, it was in the years immediately after the war that the massive migration to suburbia began. It is now both the characteristic way of life for most middle-class Americans and the best reflection of the values and aspirations of the adult generation. It is the symbolic centerpiece in the display of America's material rewards. And I think it is also the best place to look in order to understand why so many young people are trying to find new life styles.[12]

Why did so many people flee to the suburbs in the years immediately after the war? In an earlier era, workers lived on the outskirts of the cities, near the factories, while the rich lived near the city center, close to its cultural facilities. The suburban migration reversed this pattern. Suburbia promised urban convenience and rural charm, "a better place to raise the children," a separate house on a small property, and a retreat from the cities. What it delivered, of course, is something else. Most suburban communities are insular affairs, cut off from the cultural if not the economic life of nearby cities, and the promise of "rural charm" has hardly been met. But for all its unmet promises, it is important to understand why suburbia had such a strong appeal for the postwar generation, and why it continues to be the life style aspired to by those moving out of the urban ghettos or leaving small-town and rural backgrounds.

At the center of every suburban community, both literally and figuratively, is the school. The suburban version of the American Dream has this particular twist: Everything is for the children. Both social status and material abundance are to be diligently pursued, but not out of the desire for self-gratification so much as the desire to pursue these goals for the children. Suburban parents are typically preoccupied with the importance of child-raising, of putting off their own satisfactions, of moving to more desirable neighborhoods "for the kids' sake," in order that *they* can go to the best schools, enjoy safe playgrounds, have the right kinds of friends. This suburban willingness to defer life for the children's sake is so pervasive that it offers an important clue in understanding both the counter culture and the feelings of parental resentment that it kindles. The flip side of the characteristically American gaze into the future has been our disdain for tradition. Perhaps this explains why in America more than in any other country adolescence is exalted as the best years of one's life. As a nation, we've always looked to the new and the unexplored, the frontier and the future. Rather than respecting the subtle values of maturity, we celebrate the physical strength, spontaneity, and vitality of youth. Why is it, after all, that everyone over thirty is encouraged to commit cosmetic camouflage to disguise the fact? And why are the media constantly attacking us with the world view of the Now Generation? Is it because our best consumers are fairly young, or because we have no other conception of what values we might revere than those of youth? In countries where parents make fewer sacrifices for their children, there is more tolerance for those who defect from their parents' life style. The reason for so much of the rage of suburban parents whose sons and daughters defect as treasonous hippies is that they have sacrificed so much for them.

In a society that should be able to provide more leisure than any other in history, suburbia resembles modern industry in its rhythm of frantic busyness. In one of the best studies of suburbia, *Crestwood Heights,* the authors devote a whole chapter to the topic of time. Their portrait of the community stresses what anyone who lives in suburbia feels in so many different ways—compulsive activity and scheduledness:

> In Crestwood Heights time seems almost the paramount dimension of existence. . . . [the typical] wife has her own activities outside the home which are carefully scheduled. . . . The children have their school —which demands punctuality—and scheduled appointments with dentists and dancing teachers, and numerous social activities. Home life is indeed often hectic . . . schedules are so demanding that the parents feel themselves constantly impelled to inculcate the virtues of punctuality and regulating themselves and the child, at meal hour, departure for picnics, and such occasions. . . . The phenomenon which the Crestwooder calls "pressure" is caused by this concentration of demands into limited units of time. A mother will say, "I get so that I can't cope with everything." No one is more admired than the person who is "never ruffled," who keps the flow steady.[13]

All of this activity for what? Sociologists have emphasized the point that one of the crucial distinctions between the lower and the middle classes is that the first lives for "short-run hedonism," the second for "delayed gratification." The value of delaying gratification, of indefinitely postponing rewards, of denying immediate pleasure, is built into middle-class life in countless ways.

On one level, advertising conveys the message: The picture shows two carefree vacationers (*young* vacationers, of course, much younger than most of the people who could afford the vacation) frolicking in the surf, and the copy reads, "It is cool in your cottage. You hear the rustle of the ocean outside and someone is asking if anyone wants to go spearfishing. . . ." The message, of course, is that freedom, community, adventure, and uninhibited pleasure are yours for two weeks a year on your Caribbean vacation, once you decide to spend the other fifty weeks as an IBM executive in order to pay for the vacation. What many young people have done is to short-circuit the whole process, to take the themes of freedom, community, adventure, and uninhibited pleasure seriously while denying that it is necessary to go the preferred route of the IBM executive in order to get them.

On another level, the theme of deferred gratification is expressed by the Playboy Bunnies. There is a neat symbolic significance in the fact that the Playboy Clubs do their best to find (breed?) breathlessly sexy young women, and then carefully dress them (and provide ideological outfits for them in the Playboy Philosophy) in order to make the whole package nearly irresistible. Then the clubs provide the most elaborate security network to keep the clientele from getting anything more than a prurient smile.

On yet another level, deferred gratification becomes sanctified ideology, the doctrine of progress which René Dubos has characterized so well: "All societies influenced by Western civilization are at present committed to the gospel of growth—the whirling-dervish which teaches: produce more so that you can consume more so that you can produce more still. One need not be a sociologist to know that such a philosophy is insane." It is no accident that the motto of General Electric is "Progress is our most important product;" progress is one of the shibboleths of the whole American business community. Or that indefinitely postponed gratification is the suburban refrain: "Do your homework so that you'll get better grades so that you can get into a good college, which will help you to get a better job. . . ." And we all know where that train of thought leads—straight back to suburbia in the next generation.

The first law of the parents' generation, like the slogan of Louis Philippe's revolt of 1830, the bourgeois revolution, is *"Enrichissez-vous." Then* enjoy ease and luxury. But between the enticements to spend at least as quickly as you earn, and the psychological trap of not being able to change gears after you've spent half a lifetime accumulating wealth, this is an unfillable promise. As the authors of *Crestwood Heights* remark about the fate of the person who finally gains entrance to the community:

> His character will have been so firmly structured by the time he finally arrives in Crestwood Heights that leisure and inactivity are now his greatest threats. Once there, the grandchild of Irish peasants, propelled toward North America by the dream, could no more freely shed the cultural inheritance of thrift and industry, hoarding and frugality, than could the Jewish child of ghetto parentage cast off completely his age-old fear of segregation and persecution.[14]

Once set on the track of school and career, time is crucially important, and there isn't enough of it to take a "time out." "Everything," wrote Henry Miller of his childhood home, "was for tomorrow. But tomorrow never came." [15] Is it any wonder that a generation of young people who grew up in homes where there was such a premium on "keeping on the go" and deferring gratification should insist upon immediate and uncontaminated experience? The "new immediacy" encapsulates as well as any two words can the spirit of the cultural revolt. The answer of the young to all those promises of rewards "in the long run" is that in the long run people are dead.

Several years ago, in a book entitled *The American Business Creed,* the authors summarized the "values of a good society" reflected in the public statements of business leaders, industrial advertisements, and the literature of large business associations:

> Practical realism complements individualism. It stresses the importance of those problems which no adult can avoid, and it demands that each individual meet them with competence. . . . Close attention to the practical side of life demands a kind of relentless activity. . . . The emphasis on sheer activity and effort in the creed has its natural complement in high valuations of rationality, adventure, and progress.[16]

What a nice capsule statement of what the young are rebelling against: "practical realism," "those problems which no adult can avoid," "relentless activity," "rationality," and "progress." The defenders of this creed speak from many places. For example, an item that appeared in the *Albuquerque Journal* just before a two-day summer celebration of local hippies: "Police chief Felix Lujan issued a warning to hippies not to 'invade the city,' saying that he would not tolerate aimless wandering on the part of the hippies." (Despite the imprecations of Chief Lujan, the hippies have a friend at the *Albuquerque Journal.* Just below this article was a one-line filler which I quote in its entirety: "The Roman emperor Nero first persecuted the Christians.") [17]

One of the most striking features of the rural communes populated by the young who have dissented from this whole universe of assumptions is the absence of the time dimension. Because there are no clocks and no calendars, there is a great deal of time for "aimless wandering." Conversation is about the present, not the past or the future. There are no schedules, and no one will make a firm commitment for the future. Nothing is put off until tomorrow. Like the incantation of the mynah birds in Huxley's utopia, *Island*, the message is "Here and Now, Here and Now." Rejecting the world of work and deferred enjoyment, the category of play is resuscitated. Play, after all, is everything that work is not. It is immediate enjoyment, it is superfluous and unnecessary, and it is not a means to anything else. All of this by way of rejecting the parents' life style, and substituting in its place the ideals of timelessness and playfulness.

Is it really unusual that so many young people in this generation should be leaving suburbia, defecting from their parents' life style, and seeking out the alternatives? One of the most extraordinary things about the parents' generation was that so many of them were willing to shed their pasts and move to suburbia. This is one of the reasons why there is so much self-consciousness about the suburban style: For many of the participants, it is a *new* life style. Suburbia represented a solution for so many people in the postwar period because it responded to several important needs. Many people wanted to leave the complexity and diversity of the teeming cities and to find a place where the family could be more effectively insulated against the outside world. The parents' generation had peculiarly exaggerated needs for material success; suburbia provided a much better setting for the display of affluence than did urban neighborhoods. Finally, the parents' generation was preoccupied to an extraordinary extent with the kids, with having children and planning a whole life style around their needs.[18]

But the younger generation faces different problems and has different needs. They insist on living in the present, not in the future. They are much less concerned with material success and security, and the raising of children is not so important as it was for their parents. Given these needs, suburbia doesn't make any sense, and it is necessary to find alternative life styles. Perhaps it is no longer possible to expect that one generation can provide meaningful work and a way of life which most of the next generation would want to follow. But what Thoreau said, that "one generation abandons the enterprises of another like stranded vessels," is particularly true of this generation. Like the newest cars rolling off the assembly lines in Detroit, there is a kind of built-in obsolescence about suburbia. In the same way that the parents left their pasts a generation or two ago and fled to suburbia, their children are leaving and searching for an alternative.

Historically, there have been many different forms of rebellion against the conventions of the middle class, including revolutionary movements as well as withdrawal into isolated communities. It is useful to look at two movements that embodied a revolt against bourgeois culture: European Romanticism during the first half of the nineteenth century and the German Youth Movement at the turn of the century. What these movements have in common with a counter culture is an urge toward reintegration and immediacy, a rebellion against the atomistic tendencies of modern life.

The European Romantics turned away from modernity, from the advances of technology, industrial growth, and the burgeoning cities which they viewed with so much apprehension, and toward the past. They developed a nostalgia for preindustrial ages and particularly for medieval times. The Middle Ages represented everything that had been sacrificed to modernity, the transcendent concern of a knight fighting for the justice of the weak, the ballads of heroes and great deeds, the categories of the sublime and the mysterious, and the spirituality of the Church. It was an age that emphasized the ideal and the subjective rather than the real and the objective; an age which was materially poor but spiritually rich.

Yet despite this nostalgia for times past, the Romantics were not basically conservative. Both socialism and romanticism were different forms of rebellion against bourgeois culture. Both contained revolutionary elements, though of very different sorts. In several respects, the Romantics were in very much the same position as the parts of the counter culture which have rejected the possibility of effecting change through politics. The Romantics were skeptical about merely organizational reform, about the effects of simply rearranging a society's institutions. "The rejuvenation of society has never depended upon a purely political revolution," commented Charles Nodier. "It is religion which rejuvenates people." [19] The Romantics revolted not in the name of equality or to effect economic change but to enable the development of the "inner man." In this sense, they were opposed to the bourgeoisie *and* the radicals. Bourgeois conventions were rejected because they were shallow and artificial, and the radical's program of social and economic change was rejected because it did nothing to free the human spirit.

What the Romantics sought above all else was a change in the sensibilities of man, a reintegration expressed on several different levels. In this theme, the counter culture echoes the Romantics, for whom reason was at best a very inadequate means to any substantial knowledge. In the Romantic quest to encompass the whole of the universe, the quest for the infinite, it was hardly useful at all. As Coleridge wrote in one of his letters: "I have known some who have been rationally educated, as it is styled. They were marked by a microscopic acuteness, but when they looked at great things, all became blank and they saw nothing and denied (very illogically) that anything

could be seen . . . and called the want of imagination
judgment and the never being moved to rapture philosophy." [20] Rousseau had announced the theme of the rejection of reason even more clearly in his *Lettres Morales:*
"For us, to exist is to feel; and our sensibility is incontes-
tably more important than reason." [21] The exaggerated
rationalism of the eighteenth century was deposed, and in
its place the Romantics substituted a metaphysical
yearning.

Mystical union was the ultimate form of reintegration,
but the same urge was stated on another level as the desire to overcome human loneliness and separateness and
to reinstate true community. Wordsworth's rejection of
the inhumanities of modern industrial cities was typical:

> . . . he truly is alone,
> He of the multitude whose eyes are doomed
> To hold a vacant commerce day by day
> With objects wanting life,
>   repelling love
> Where pity shrinks from unremitting calls,
> Where numbers overwhelm humanity,
> And neighborhood serves rather to divide
> Than to unite. . . .[22]

Corollary to this rejection of city life was the exalting
of nature, Wordsworth's enthusiasm for the "tranquil sub-
limity" of the Lake District and his belief in the sacredness of all living things.

All the symptoms of the Romantic attitude, the affirma-
tion of the spiritual, the reliance on intuition, a fierce
insistence on the subjective and the ideal, as well as disenchantment, apocalyptic fervor, and defiance of bourgeois conventions—that is, the sensibility which the Romantics and the counter culture share—are much more
compatible with youth than middle age. "To live beyond
forty," said Dostoyevsky's underground diarist, "is bad

taste." And this was especially so for the Romantics, so many of whom either had meteoric careers before fading into middle age, or in fact died young.

Perhaps the reason why the German Youth Movement at the turn of the century which revived the romantic quest for integration and immediacy was so frequently on the hysteric fringe of the Romantic tradition is due as much to its extreme youthfulness as to its specifically Germanic overtones.[23] In a much more direct sense than the Romantics, the school-age youths who participated in the German Youth Movement explicitly rejected almost all the conventions of German society. As an oppositional movement that began with virtually no program, but was propelled by an almost total rejection of contemporary society, the German Youth Movement is more familiar to us than the Romantics. In its early years, it was completely nonideological, not so much a movement as a set of shared attitudes that included attacks on the bookishness and bureaucracy of the schools, authoritarianism at home, the impotence of governmental leaders, and the ugliness of industrial towns. Like the Romantics, the German Youth Movement looked to the past for a solution. As Peter Pulzer has stated it:

> The more Germany was covered with slag heaps, slum tenements, and giant office blocks, the more tantalizing became her rivers and forests, her ruined castles and half-timbered townships. The more the average German was a slave to his wages and his mortgage, the more attracted he was to his mythical ancestor, the heroic warrior-peasant, loyal to his tribe, protector of his womenfolk, obedient to his chieftain.[24]

Nature was important, but not in the way that it had been for the Romantics. Mystical for Wordsworth, nature for the German youths posed a challenge and a physical task. Camping in the forests and hills was popular because of the fellowship of facing danger together. Like the communal movement in the counter culture, the answer to the softness and corruption of bourgeois life was not just to escape to nature, but to exalt a hard primitivism. And like the nature-food cult within the counter culture, the German youths were emphatic about the importance of various "life reform" gestures such as protests against the use of tobacco and alcohol.

Very much in the tradition of the Romantics, the German Youth Movement represented the fusion of cultural criticism with the denigration of rationality. "I have no use for abstract truth," announced one of its leaders, "I want to bind and liberate my people." [25] This is the recurring formula of mystical liberation, so different from the liberal notion of liberty and autonomy: Psychic liberation comes only at the price of fusion, of total unity. This desire for an all-encompassing faith, for a totally absorbing community of believers, finally became a tyrannical ideal for the German Youth Movement. What started as a very loosely organized band of hikers and nature enthusiasts became in 1913 a union called the Free German Youth, consisting of about fifty thousand members. By 1914, part of the movement was radicalized. Not long afterward, Hitler provided a haven for many of the same people: The Nazi party was both an all-encompassing faith and a totally absorbing community. Certainly at this point the similarities between the German Youth Movement and the counter culture can easily be exaggerated. Both share a concern for dethroning reason as "the prime enchantress," and in turn celebrate the nonrational. But it is the most unfortunate historical accident that the most recent surge of intuitionism should have taken its worst possible form as Nazism. The critical difference between the intuitionism of the German Youth Movement and the counter culture is that in Germany it was linked with a cult of messianic leadership, while in the counter culture there is a pervasive fear of leadership in any form.

Despite these differences, there is at least one other intriguing similarity between the German Youth Movement and the counter culture. The German youths faced a crucial problem which every other oppositional movement has had to solve. For them, as well as the Russian student movement at the turn of the century and the counter culture, "the Great Refusal" implied a total rejection of almost every aspect of the mainstream bourgeois culture. When Fanon dismissed the bourgeois epoch as "a completely useless phase," he was speaking specifically to the Third World. Yet when he voiced his revulsion at the bourgeoisie, which, "expressing its mediocrity in its profits, its achievements, and in its thought tries to hide this mediocrity by buildings which have prestige value at the individual level, by chromium plating on big American cars, by holidays on the Riviera, and weekends in neon-lit nightclubs," [26] he is expressing the same disenchantment with the middle-class ethos that is embodied in each of these oppositional movements. Looking for some alternative to the bourgeois style, the German Youth Movement reached back to its past, to the ideal of mythical ancestors, in much the same way that the Romantics idealized the Middle Ages. But this search for a life style that they could affirm led them more importantly back to "the people," the peasants who were still living close to the land, the intrinsically German folk. Predictably, this attraction to the peasantry never developed into a firm alliance. For all their vague notions of solidarity with the folk, the German youths did not remain for long among the peasants, nor did they take up political issues on their behalf. What the peasants provided was both an example and a symbol which sharpened the German

Youth Movement's dissent against the mainstream society, against modernity, the industrialized city, and "progress."

What has happened in the counter culture is very similar, even if the problem of finding peasants or natives whose lives have not been infiltrated by bourgeois culture is much more difficult now than it was for the German or the Russian youth movements. What are the surviving indigenous life styles in this country which offer an alternative to middle-class culture? In New England and the Northwest, the best that this culture can provide is the life style of rural areas and isolated small towns. But in the Southwest, and especially in New Mexico, which was the center of the first large communal migration, there is an ideal solution to this problem of finding an authentic peasantry. The American Indian tribes come as close to a peasant class as any group in this country. And at least in many of the communes in the Taos area, the middle-class young have adopted not just the adobe huts and farming techniques of the Indians but their religion as well.

Like the Romantics and the German Youth Movement, this contemporary assault on middle-class conventions involves a rejection of urban civilization and an attempt at reintegration and immediacy. Playfulness and timelessness are by no means the only expressions of this new immediacy. It takes many other forms, most of which were anticipated by the Romantics; for example, nature mysticism, the absolute submergence of self in community, or the insistence upon uncontaminated sensual experience. But of all these manifestations of the new immediacy, the psychedelic experience is closest to the mystic ideal and the most potent catalyst for the new sensibility. Typically, the drug-inspired mystic recovers perceptual innocence: The mind, which normally is so busy making distinctions among things, is silenced. Time and space become profoundly inconsequential, along with all other categories, concepts, rules, schedules, and obligations. Mystic union is that state in which subject-object distinctions dissolve. Suddenly the windows of perception are cleansed, the self melts into the whole universe, and everything shimmers in its pristine unity. As Aldous Huxley reported what he felt during his first experience with mescaline, "This is how one ought to see, how things really are. . . . If one always saw like this, one would never want to do anything else. Just looking, just being . . . that would be enough." [27] This contemplative state stands in absolute opposition to the active, self-assertive, cognitive mode. Once converted to this timeless realm, the claims of everyday reality seem fraudulent indeed.

What seems most fraudulent is the WASP idiom of responsibility and self-restraint, and it is this style which is bearing the brunt of the attack. If we had to describe the prototypical American male, he probably wouldn't be too different from the composite picture of the astronauts. The names of the space programs—Mercury, Gemini, Apollo—reach back to Roman mythology and conjure up images of fantastic voyages and superhuman quests. But the astronauts themselves are by and large unadulterated, crewcut, narrow-tie, family-style, mainstream Americana. No heroes, they are just-the-facts-please men. But then, there's no place for an identity crisis in the flight plans. The script calls for low-profile dispassionate blandness. As someone at the Houston Space Center said about Neil Armstrong after his carefully preplanned speech on the moon, "He surprised us. Yes or no from him is a big conversation." For all the public-relations consciousness of the program and for all our paeans to the melting pot, the space program is one of the last bastions of WASP hegemony, as well as the best expression of the WASP idiom. The astronauts are exemplary cases of what Kenneth Keniston called the "technological ego." [28] The desired personality type—and not just in the space program —is a person who will function without high idealism, who will substitute a realistic and practical outlook. Cognition and rationality take precedence over feeling and fantasy. Know-how triumphs over knowing why. The most important thing is a "zero-defects" job.

According to Freud, the edifice of civilization is built upon repression of the instinctual life. We pay the price of our inhibitions for the material securities which civilization provides. In the counter culture, of course, both Freud and the astronauts are emphatically rejected. As opposed to the subdued WASP style, the new aesthetic celebrates texture, a high-decibel assault on the ears, a Day-Glo assault on the eyes. The WASP style was reflected in the remarkably unimaginative names which parents gave to their children. Since it was important to choose a name both bland and proper, there were forty million Roberts and Timothys, Susans and Janes. To correct the deficiency, names as well as identities are frequently changed in the counter culture. And the names that people take reflect the contours and preoccupations of the new sensibility as surely as the names that their parents chose reflected theirs. One of the minor heroes of the counter culture, Hugh Romney in his former life, is now Wavy Gravy. Bill Wheeler, one of the communal pioneers in California, is the father of a new baby called Raspberry Sundown Hummingbird Wheeler. The names run through the metaphysical spectrum—Krishna, Ishmael, Ovid, and Turtle. No button-down low-profile WASPS here.

The premise of the new immediacy is that society demands many more sacrifices than necessary, that its repressions of the instinctual life are excessive and dysfunctional. This was Allen Ginsberg's point in the most

eloquent testimony given at the Chicago Trial when he
explained the meaning of the Festival of Life:

> As part of our nature, we have many loves, many of
> which are suppressed, many of which are denied,
> many of which we deny to ourselves. [Whitman] said
> that the reclaiming of those lives and the becoming
> aware of those loves was the only way this nation could
> save itself and become a democratic and spiritual
> republic. He said that unless there was an infusion of
> feeling, of tenderness, of fearlessness, of spirituality,
> of natural sexuality, of natural delight in each other's
> bodies, into the hardened, materialistic, cynical, life-
> denying, clearly competitive, afraid, scared, armored
> bodies, there would be no chance for spiritual democ-
> racy to take root in America.

Judge Julius J. Hoffman, always a marvelous caricature
of the worst of the mainstream culture, evidently wanted
nothing to do with a spiritual democracy. When Ralph
Abernathy and defense attorney William Kunstler
greeted each other on the courtroom floor with effusive
hugging, an offended Judge Hoffman huffed that he had
"never seen so much physical affection in a courtroom."

In any revolutionary era when old assumptions are
discarded, words are among the first casualties. As soon
as the counter culture enters there is a blizzard of quo-
tation marks around words which only yesterday provided
the firm communality of our discourse. The suspicion is
that reason and words are the opiate of the masses, that
they bind us to the status quo. In another age in which
reason was displaced by intuition and passion, George
Sorel stated, "Words matter little to those who wish to
get at the root of things." [29] Thus Abbie Hoffman is for
once part of an identifiable tradition when he says, "Don't
rely on words. Words are the absolute in horseshit."

As with many of the other characteristics of the counter culture, its rejection of words begins with a fundamental insight which pierces through one of the most encrusted assumptions of the West—that reason is the best part of man and the only way of knowing. But in its impatience to dethrone reason, something of considerable value is rejected entirely. Rather than attempting to free words and concepts from the distortion that is inflicted when military atrocities are camouflaged by smoke screens like "escalation" and "deterrence," it assumes that all words are false. In its eagerness to unmask the free-lance minds ready to work for the highest bidders and perpetrate a very dangerous kind of "objectivity," the counter culture concludes that there is no knowledge, only the sociology of knowledge, only inhuman motives masquerading in the depersonalized euphemisms of the experts. Since in the mainstream culture there are so many conceptual filters between man and experience, since sensations are classified before they are experienced, conceptualization, classification, analysis, and explanation are eschewed altogether.

The result is an antagonism to intellect in any form. This is an unfortunate distortion of the original impulse of the New Left, which was not to attack the world of ideas, but simply to dethrone reason as the sole means of knowing. Ideally, the task of reason is to tidy up inchoate sensations, to make some sense out of experience. But it has become increasingly obvious that the barbarisms of science unchecked by intuition are at least as great as those of experience and intuition unchecked by reason. The cloak of "objectivity" disguises the most inhuman motives. The tenor of the counter culture on this point is reflected well in a statement which appears in the catalog of New York's Free University: "Passionate involvement, intellectual confrontation and clash of ideas are particularly encouraged because we believe that a

detached search for ideas and a dispassionate, objective
position do not, and have never existed." But predictably
a university, even a free university, has certain problems
when students are long on intuition and short on reason
and discipline. Joseph Berke, an instructor at the Free
University who gave a course entitled "The Psychotic
Experience as an Archetype of Paradise Lost," commented that when the participants talked about their own
experiences, the meetings went very well. "But it was
very difficult to try to hold a discussion on material not
immediately personal, but which people had to read up
on the week before the meeting. This difficulty was common to all classes at FUNY and bugged the faculty no
end. It was almost as if people needed the whip of exams
before they would approach the subject matter." [30]

The catalogs of alternative universities are haphazard
collections in which the sacred and the profane, the inconsequential, the scatological, the portentous, and the
sublime are all mixed together. The underground papers
reflect this same delight in smashing the categories that
insist that some things are more important than others.
The result is creation by indeterminacy, the art of the
collage in which elements of experience governed by different principles are juxtaposed, what Lewis Carroll was
concerned with when he spoke "Of shoes—and ships—
and sealing wax— / Of cabbages—and kings." Like the
theater of Antonin Artaud, which seeks to "explore our
nervous impressionability with rhythms, sounds, words,
resonances, and vocalisations," [31] most of these new art
forms are concerned to assail our sensibilities rather than
arousing our thought. The Romantic genius was best
translated in music; similarly, the best of the new art
forms are those which rely upon intuition and emotion.
The new music explores the uncharted realms of the expressive range. Religious innovations such as the new
liturgies reflect an understanding of the religious essence

that the God-is-dead theologians completely missed. At
its best, the new theater is brilliantly iconoclastic in shak-
ing up the conventions of proscenium theater.

But the new sensibility is at its worst in words and
thought. One of the most energetic proponents of creation by indeterminacy, John Cage, once commented to a
colleague, "You have a beautiful mind, but I think it's
time you threw it away." Looking at most of the underground papers, I think that is exactly what has happened.
The titles demonstrate a certain exuberant idiosyncracy:
At last count, the underground press included such delights as *Kiss, Probe,* and *Fusion; The Ungarbled Word,
Seventy Nine Cent Spread, The Jones Family Grand-
children, Fatigue Press, The American Dream* and *Ptero-
dactyl* ("Hatched in Beautifull Grinnell, Iowa"). But the
titles are more interesting than the contents. Most of them
consist of the endless repetition of slogans, which are a
deceptive excuse for not thinking. Want an answer? Plug
in your favorite slogan: Peace, Brotherhood, Love, or
Fascist Pig. All of it useful in roughly the same way that
Couéism was useful in France, when hundreds of thousands were endlessly repeating "Day by day, in every
way, I am getting better and better." That is, a certain
self-hypnotic value, but useless as a substitute for thinking. All in all, the underground papers demonstrate a
noisy emptiness; they're more useful as a reflection of
what the counter culture is than as a comprehension of
what it's all about.

But perhaps this is understandable since the underground journalists are the heirs to Jack Kerouac's "spontaneous prose" style. He had one rule, a self-imposed "no
revision" rule. His method was to place a roll of paper in
the typewriter and bang out eight or nine feet a day. As
Kerouac explained, he would make no alterations because
"whatever you try to delete . . . that's what's most interesting to a doctor." Which makes sense if your reader is

a psychiatrist and is absurd if not. The underground writers follow his method, but since most of them lack his talent, the writing is constantly on the verge of irrelevant narcissism. Impatient with complexity and the demands of coherence, the new sensibility wants works of literature that, in Irving Howe's memorable words, "will be as absolute as the sun, as unarguable as orgasm, and as delicious as a lollipop." [32]

The new immediacy is an important criticism of the old pieties of self-restraint, the production ethic, and the indefinitely postponed life, but it is a sensibility that has all the faults of its virtues. Rejecting the frenzied activity of their parents, many of the communal young substitute an exaggerated passivity, a nearly catatonic do-nothing-ness. Reacting to the empty disciplines of their parents' lives, they resort to programmatic hostility toward any order, the rejection of every requirement of competence, and the assumption that all forms of imperatives are "repressive." Too often, the Great Refusal is nothing more than refusal.

But this, obviously, is too harsh a judgment. To assume that within a few short years the young could reverse all their parents' most entrenched assumptions, explore the alternatives, and invent a coherent life style is surely to assume too much.

5 : *The Anarchist Response*

> Manipulated for national goals they cannot believe
> in, the young are alienated. On every continent there
> is excessive urbanization and the world is headed
> toward ecological disaster. Under these conditions, the
> young reject authority, for it is not only immoral, but
> functionally incompetent. They are in an historical
> situation to which anarchism is the only possible
> response.
>
> —Paul Goodman

One of the curious facts about the communal movement
is that the most detailed contemporary blueprint of what
an alternative society might look like, B. F. Skinner's
Walden Two, has been disregarded in all but a handful
of communities. But to say that it has been "disregarded"
is to put it too mildly. Despite Skinner's unexceptionable
desire to create a society which is radically different from
our own, the one that he created elicits a nearly unanimous hostility from the counter culture. If it is difficult
to describe the characteristics that hundreds of communes have in common, it is easier to say what they are
not. Even if this repeats a very counter-cultural trait—to
define oneself in contradiction to a given model—it is a
useful place to begin, because in every important respect

the anarchist style of the communes stands in marked opposition to Skinner's utopia.

Most utopias begin as vehicles for criticism of the existing society, and Skinner's is no exception. Plato wrote the *Republic* hoping to reform Athens. Thomas More's *Utopia*, critical of the social ills of the time, was written in the hope of influencing Henry VIII. Skinner begins with a critique of a society which teaches moribund competitiveness, in which the isolated family is increasingly weak and vulnerable, in which children grow up to be selfish, exploitative, and gluttonous.

In *Walden Two* he formulates a radical alternative, a contrasting image of what society might be like. Using the partial disguise of the literary form, utopian writers have advocated the most revolutionary changes imaginable. When manual work was considered degrading, utopian writers reasserted its dignity. During an era of sacrosanct private property, there have been many utopian advocates of a community of goods. Aldous Huxley proposed the widespread use of "Moksha" in his island utopia in the early sixties when all forms of drug use were in official disrepute. In this sense, utopias have found a lively market among the young who are looking for alternatives. Huxley's *Island* has run through a dozen printings and more than half a million copies. And *Walden Two* has had an even more spectacular success. First published in 1948, it was ahead of its time and not very popular for several years. In the years since, it has attracted more and more attention. At least a million copies have now been printed.

Like an ideology, a utopia is in some sense a call to action. The embryonic literary utopias of Etienne Cabet, Fourier, and Owen, to mention just a few, are all schemes that men have seriously tried to translate into practice. Like many utopian writers, Theodor Hertzka, a distinguished Viennese economist whose *Freeland* first appeared in 1889, argued that his fiction might be turned into fact:

> For this book is not the idle creation of an uncontrolled imagination, but the outcome of earnest, sober reflection, and of profound scientific investigation. All that I have described as really happening *might* happen if men were found who, convinced as I am of the untenability of existing conditions, determined to act instead of merely complaining. . . . There is no longer anything to compel us to endure the misery of an obsolete system; there is nothing but our own folly to prevent us from enjoying that happiness and abundance which the existing means of civilization are capable of providing for us.[1]

Like *Island* and *Walden Two, Freeland* met a very enthusiastic reception. Within a few years after it appeared there were almost a thousand local Freeland societies with the intention of putting Hertzka's plan into effect. His followers even purchased a tract of land in British East Africa and sent an expedition of volunteers there before the whole experiment foundered on practical problems.

There is nothing in *Walden Two* that is any more difficult to translate into practice than *Freeland* was. In the decades since its publication, there have been several groups that have worked toward a scientifically designed and operated community such as Walden Two. At least one of them, a scaled-down model in the farmlands of central Virginia, is a faithful attempt to make Skinner's dream come true. The Twin Oaks community feels more like a farm than the semi-industrial town which Skinner proposed, but despite some concessions to hip culture, Skinner's presence is felt. Jobs are allocated according to a labor-credit system. There is an elected board of planners, and managers for such tasks as community health maintenance, the vegetable garden, and hammock-

making (one of the community's profit-making industries). Unlike many of the hip communes that exalt drug
mysticism, Twin Oaks outlaws pot because of the possibility of police harassment. And there are such Skin-
nerian touches as the use of M & M's as rewards (or, as
they prefer, "reinforcers") for noticing violations of item
nine in the Twin Oaks code, which says that members
will clean up after themselves. But this is only one commune among hundreds. From the point of view of most
of the young people dropping out of the mainstream and
into communes, Twin Oaks is at best an unattractive
alternative.

So what is it about Skinner's model that makes it so
unsuitable to the counter culture? *Walden Two* is the
story of a visit by a professor named Burris to an experimental community planned by Frazier, a former student of his. The community is based on the assumption
that man is *not* free, that through careful "cultural engineering" man's behavior can be shaped to allow him the
greatest possible happiness. The premise that Skinner's
critics have attacked most heatedly is that the best behavior for the individual is that which promotes the Good
Life of the group. The social whole is more important
than the individual parts.

The community consists of a carefully designed experiment in which any condition or event that influences
behavior is controlled so that it has the desired effect. Infants are protected from unnecessary discomforts and
annoyances in cubicles which are air-conditioned
and noiseless. The behavior of young children is shaped
according to the results of experimental study, never according to the revelations of "good conduct." Education
stresses self-control and the prevention of envy, jealousy,
and fear. As Skinner explains it, the result is control without the use of force: "By a careful design we control not
the final behavior, but the inclination to behave—the mo-

tives, the desires, the wishes. . . . They are doing what
they want to do, not what they are forced to do. . . . It's
not control that's lacking when one feels free, but the
objectionable control of force."

All this careful cultural engineering nearly obviates
conflict and the necessity of politics. The community is
governed by a rotating board of planners, but since people are trained for co-operative behavior very little control
is necessary. Repeating a suggestion which has occurred again and again in the utopian literature, Skinner
abolishes the division of labor. Like everyone else in the
community, the planners have to work out some of their
labor credits by doing menial tasks. Everyone has the
responsibility and the obligation to develop his full powers, physical and intellectual. In Walden Two, unnecessary tasks as well as superfluous possessions are avoided.
Such labor-saving innovations as the "industrialization of
housewifery" are made in order to reduce to an absolute
minimum the number of undesirable jobs. As a consequence, community members have to work only four
hours a day, and have abundant leisure time.

Near the end of the book, Frazier looks out over his
creation and remarks to Burris, "Practically all of Walden
Two can be seen from here. . . . There's Morrison at the
piggery again. More inoculations, I presume. And over
here—a load of early kale going into the poultry house.
. . . And there's the mailman nudging his old Ford over
the hill. . . . There's old Mrs. Ackerman out for a walk
again. And that must be Esther with her." Obviously the
meditations of a man feeling sort of misty about the
whole thing. Yet this bit of neo-*Our Town* somehow mis-
carries disastrously. The result of all that cultural engineering is synthetic happiness, lobotomized man with his
taste for freedom excised. George Orwell once commented
that "happiness is notoriously difficult to describe, and
pictures of a just and well-ordered society are seldom

either attractive or convincing." [2] He is certainly right in this case. What Skinner has created is a universe in which people seem hardly to move and breathe, in which no one would get up in the middle of the night for a sandwich. But the claustrophobia of Skinner's utopia results from more than his clumsiness as a novelist, his failure to create flesh-and-blood characters. Part of it owes to the fact that Skinner has conceived of a perfect society in which cultural engineering has succeeded in eliminating struggle, trial, and conflict. In this rarefied atmosphere our whole ethical tradition, concerned above all else with what man does with his freedom, collapses. All homogenized and pasteurized, most of the highest forms of human achievement are laughable here. *War and Peace* written by a member of the Walden Two community after four stimulating hours of work in an efficient and pleasant little community? Absurd. Perhaps this is the reason why the utopias never have as much literary interest as the anti-utopias such as *Brave New World* and *1984*.

There is already a very sizable literature damning Skinner, and there is no particular virtue in adding to it. [3] But it is important to understand why Skinner's critics have been so adamant, and particularly why *Walden Two* is so unacceptable to the counter culture. His motives in writing the book were, after all, nearly impeccable. What he suggested was that through conditioning, rather than shame, fear, or punishment, we might create

> a world in which there is food, clothing, and shelter for all, where everyone chooses his own work and works on the average only four hours a day, where music and the arts flourish, where personal relationships develop under the most favorable circumstances, where education prepares every child for the social and intellectual life before him, where—in short— people are truly happy, secure, productive, creative, and forward-looking. [4]

One of the criticisms of Skinner has been that, despite the words which he put into Frazier's mouth—"You've got to experiment, and experiment with your own life. Not just sit back . . . in an ivory tower somewhere as if your own life weren't mixed up in it"—he never tested his ideas in a real community, and has carefully kept his distance from the Walden Two-influenced communities such as Twin Oaks.[5] But you don't necessarily ask the man who crushes the grapes to serve the wine, and certainly this objection doesn't explain much of the hostility toward *Walden Two*.

Skinner himself partially explained that hostility when he commented:

> If these critics had come upon a society in some remote corner of the world which boasted similar advantages, they would undoubtedly have hailed it as providing a pattern which we all might well follow— providing that it was the clear result of a natural process of cultural evolution. Any evidence that intelligence had been used in arriving at this version of the good life would, in their eyes, be a serious flaw.[6]

This is undoubtedly part of the reason why *Walden Two* has had so little influence on the communal movement. In the same way that the counter culture rejects *any* completely defined doctrinal system, it rejects all utopias of the traditional sort that specify every detail of the social order. In the performance of guerrilla theater, for example, there is no script that determines a formal beginning, middle, and end. Similarly, this resistance to closure is expressed in the feeling that the only revolutionary more dangerous than the one who has no idea of what the postrevolutionary society should be like is the one who comes with a completed blueprint under his arm.

But there is a more important objection than this, and

one that explains the preference for anarchist communities. Skinner is both a faithful heir to the utopian tradition and the last of the utopians. One of the consistent utopian themes since Plato's *Republic* has been a belief in external compulsion, in strict laws and binding institutions. Plato distrusted the emotional life and had a limited faith in the judgment of the average person. Denying that each man should be his own ruler, he instituted a ruling class of benevolent guardians invested with the power to govern the masses. Ever since, most utopias have been rigid and authoritarian. The assumption has been that the best way of maintaining the good society is through law and a profusion of regulatory details. Like a mother so intent upon her child's well-being that she suffocates it with her attention, most of the utopias sink under the weight of too many restrictions and an obsessive desire to protect against the unforeseen and the accidental. The fatal flaw of so many of the utopian writers is that they imagined that the perfect society would be like a perfectly ordered, smoothly running machine. As Tocqueville remarked of those whose "love of order is indistinguishable from their partiality to tyrants," most of the utopians have concluded that the price of conflict and disorder is too great, and that the only alternative is the authoritarian state.

This passion for order at the expense of freedom is satirized in the anti-utopias of *Brave New World, 1984,* and Zamyatin's *We.* Zamyatin portrays life in the Unique State, ruled by the Benefactor and his agents, the Guardians, who keep the citizens under constant surveillance. Since men are not worthy of freedom, privacy is denied and life is regulated with a mathematical precision. Everyone is required to wear a conspicuous gold plate bearing his number. On the other side of this gold plate is the watch by which each citizen is integrated into the mechanism of the society. Every room has a timetable, and work, sleep, eating, and sexual intercourse are all strictly regulated. Freedom is not only unnecessary in the Unique State, but dangerous.

Like Huxley and Zamyatin, George Orwell wrote an anti-utopia which in its boundless despair forecast the excesses not only of Communism subverted to totalitarianism but of *all* threats to individual freedom. Significantly, *1984* was published just a year after Skinner's *Walden Two*. And what Orwell wrote of Zamyatin's *We*, that it deals "with the rebellion of the primitive human spirit against a rationalized, mechanized, painless world," could as well be said of his own book.[7]

Huxley accuses society of wanting security and stability so much that it is willing to dispense entirely with individual freedom. His criticism of the meticulously organized authoritarian utopias is that their creators, like Skinner, are constantly willing to subordinate the individual to the well-being of the social organism. In the Brave New World, we trade in *Liberté, Égalité,* and *Fraternité* and get in return Community, Identity, and Stability. In the rugged days of the previous regime, those who had freedom were claiming the right to God, to poetry, to goodness, perhaps, but they were also claiming the right to be unhappy, "not to mention the right to grow old and ugly and impotent," said the World Controller, "the right to have syphilis and cancer; the right to live in constant apprehension of what may happen tomorrow; the right to catch typhoid, the right to be tortured by unspeakable pains of every kind."[8] Since unorthodoxy threatens society itself, in the Brave New World the decanting process in the human hatchery assures a calculated orthodoxy. Order is sustained not by force but by genetic control, pharmacological manipulation, and psychological surveillance. The key to happiness is consumption and drug-induced stupefaction.

For all the ways in which the anti-utopias of this century have warned against excessive authority, many of the utopias of the eighteenth and nineteenth centuries were in fact antidotes to disorder. In the eighteenth century, the preoccupation with uniformity and consistent regulations reflected a desire to be rid of a chaotic mess of conflicting legal and institutional structures. In the nineteenth century, an era of unbridled individualism, social Darwinism, and the-less-government-the-better politics, utopian writers envisioned a vast administrative network which would ensure the smooth running of society and the material well-being of everyone. Utopias suggested such radical innovations as the welfare state, government-provided health care, and unemployment insurance.

But one of the reasons why utopia has such a bad name for itself now is that in many ways we are living the utopias of the past, and they have not lived up to their promise. Edward Bellamy's *Looking Backward,* a utopian romance written in the 1880's, anticipated the triumphant socialist state of A.D. 2000 in which an aristocracy of experts successfully pilots the society through the technical maze and delivers fabulous quantities of consumer goods. The price? Just twenty-one years of compulsory education and twenty-four years of conscripted labor, which Bellamy considered a reasonable demand for the state to make. Features of Bellamy's utopia such as the nationalization of industry and the dominance of the managerial class are already familiar to us. We would hail him as a first-rate prophet, except that he hardly anticipated what life in his utopia would *feel* like. In the twentieth century we have experienced all-powerful states which have carried out Bellamy's utopian plan, which have encouraged scientific discoveries and stimulated productive capacities. But we have also seen that affluence gives rise to new inequalities, that people are slaves to the productive process and tied to pleasureless consumption, and that totalitarian states have outlawed individual thought as heresy. We might better heed the prophecy of Nicholas Berdyaev:

> Utopias appear to be much more capable of realization than they did in the past. And we find ourselves faced by a much more distressing problem: How can we prevent their final realization? . . . Utopias can be realized. Life advances toward utopia. And perhaps a new century is beginning, a century in which the intellectuals and the cultivated classes will dream of the means by which utopias can be avoided, and how we can return to a non-utopian society, less "perfect" and more free.[9]

If many of the utopias of the past were antidotes to disorder, the lesson of the anti-utopias and the last half-century is that it is not disorder but too much order which threatens our society. It is in this context that the attempt to revive the anarchist tradition makes sense. In a society that still justifies centralism in the name of efficiency and a profusion of regulatory details as necessary concessions to the complexity of modern life, the anarchist task is to dismantle as many forms of dysfunctional authority and oppression as possible. Unlike most of the utopians, the anarchists stress freedom rather than order: their consistent theme is an emphasis on the unhindered natural development of the individual. Man is essentially good, but he has been warped by political, religious, educational, and economic institutions. The anarchist assumption is that the only legitimate form of regulation is self-regulation. External authority of any kind is illegitimate. In Proudhon's words, "Whoever lays his hands on me to govern me is a usurper and a tyrant; I declare him to be my enemy." Or even more simply, in the words of the Australian anarchist Harry Hooten, "All handling of man is manhandling."

The liberal regards institutions as the safeguards of

personal liberty; the anarchist regards them as a threat to freedom, as repressive authority. As opposed to the treacherous ideal of "law and order," the anarchist argues that the only viable order results from the spontaneous, voluntary cooperation of individuals within the social organism. Since law is an external constraint, it inhibits self-regulation and is therefore morally illegitimate. Anarchism means life without government. For all the differences among the anarchist writers, the common assumption is that men are naturally good, that if they are placed in an environment where they are not corrupted by institutions or meddling authority they can live together harmoniously and will work spontaneously for the good of the whole society.

The popular image of anarchism is, of course, very different from this benign vision of a society of harmonious cooperation. "In the popular mind," said Bertrand Russell, "an anarchist is a person who throws bombs and commits other outrages, either because he is more or less insane, or because he uses the pretense of extreme political opinions as a cloak for criminal proclivities." [10] The violent hatred expressed by anarchists such as Alexander Berkman, who attempted to assassinate the industrialist Henry Clay Frick as an "act of liberation" in the interest of the oppressed working class, expresses the negative aspect of the tradition. Yet Berkman himself as an older man stated its positive aspect, the emphasis upon new human relationships:

> If your object is to secure liberty, you must learn to do without authority and compulsion. If you intend to live in peace and harmony with your fellow men, you and they should cultivate brotherhood and respect for each other. If you want to work together with them for your mutual benefit, you must practice cooperation. The social revolution means much more than the reorganization of conditions only: it means

> the establishment of new human values and social re-
> lationships, a changed attitude of man to man, as of
> one free and independent to his equal. It means a
> different spirit in individual and collective life, and
> that spirit cannot be born overnight.[11]

While there is no more consistency in the anarchism of
the counter culture than there has been among the anarchist writers, most of the communes are deliberate experiments in leaderlessness, in erasing boundaries and
eliminating rules. If it is impossible to get back to the
Garden, to a state of simplicity and integral harmony, it
is quite possible to shed most of the accumulated authoritarian baggage. As Gridley Wright, the founder of one of
the early communes, put it: "I kind of laid down that
there would be no structure. There would be complete
acceptance of everybody's trip, simply because I found
the more I had been able to accept MYSELF and the
people around me, and the more they were able to accept
me, the higher we got. I wanted to see a whole community where this could happen." [12]

E. H. Carr once commented that anarchism in the nineteenth century was a critique of society, not a plan for
social reconstruction. The anarchist ideal of doing without government was conceived as a corrective to the
emerging industrial order, but it was difficult for anarchists to imagine a society that had a life of its own. Like
any party out of power, the anarchists enjoyed the luxury
of never having to prove their rhetoric in practice. But
the anarchist communes in the counter culture are in a
very different position; every one of them has to face the
practical problem of maintaining a community which is
leaderless and unstructured, in which people practice
the new human values and relationships which Berkman
spoke of.

One of the first of these communal experiments was

Lou Gottlieb's Morningstar Ranch. Gottlieb, a folk singer with the pop group The Limelighters, spent part of his show-business fortune in 1966 to buy a thirty-two-acre apple orchard in Sonoma County, north of San Francisco. His idea was that, with no rules and no organization, everyone could be reborn to live in harmony with the earth. Articulate, serene, and ingeniously simple, when Gottlieb talks about the idea it seems not just possible, but inevitable. "People live here according to the tablets written on the human heart. Once you've abandoned materialistic goals and incentives you develop a very different attitude toward things. A hippie is someone who won't work for things, security, and status. Labor done without a real purpose, in the words of the Bible, is service to Mammon, not man. I'm a hippie, a white man, and dropped out. I'm possibly a reincarnated American Indian. I live much like the California Indians did a hundred years ago. I live the way this land calls for me to live. The message is that any hour can be the last. Let's make every hour meaningful. Let's not pass our days sitting next to a guy in the Stock Exchange with a spastic colon who's always going to go sailing in the future, play with his kids tomorrow, never conscious or appreciative of what he's doing now.

"This community is a place for people to find the kind of work they'd be doing whether or not they got paid for it," he continued. "In short, your own thing, the abandonment of materialist values. I believe one of the major problems of our time is to teach people to do nothing. I can't do it yet. That is the highest form of consciousness, the fourth stage of Jnana yoga, the yoga of philosophy. The United States is artificially populated by the most competitive people, because all the contemplatives were left behind in Europe. Americans are all Karma yogas, people who literally can't sit still. My mother, if she came upon an catatonic schizoid, would scream at him to get busy. I got that until it absolutely deformed my childhood. It was never enough just to sit and scratch your balls, enjoying yourself.

"Everything we do is hurting Mother—Mother Nature, that is. Marx is meaningless because the ultimate source of profit is Mother. The function of intentional communities is for people to find their own natural activity with as little pressure as possible. It's no good for you to be telling people this is OK and that is wrong, telling others to stop whatever they're doing. You've got to change yourself first if anything around you is going to change.

"The idea of Morningstar is new—it's an *open* intentional community. No one is denied access to the land. If you have land from which nobody can be told to split, then the land selects the people. Those who don't work hard can't survive. The vibrations of the land always protect the community."

The first to come to Gottlieb's land were city people, fed up with concrete and gasoline fumes. At the beginning, there were a few dozen people who built modest shelters of canvas and wood among the trees, planted gardens, and picked the fruit. And then more and more people came, freaks looking for a place to get cooled out of their amphetamine anxieties, and bikers roaring down the roads of Sonoma County looking for Gottlieb's apple orchards. By the summer of 1967, the semiresidents were already swamped by the transients. One Saturday late in July, three hundred people showed up for dinner.

But through it all, Gottlieb stuck to his original belief and pleaded with people to respect the land. "Inevitably, when you get a good group of people together the vibes go up, and there's a lot of love going around. Then all the loveless show up and immediately you're forced into making a choice. Either accept everyone or develop criteria to figure out who's worthy. In a closed community, those who aren't worthy get bounced, but it's the bouncer who is killing himself. There have been a few cases where we've had to ask people to go, but it's at a terrible, terrible cost to everybody's soul that this is done. That's artificial selection which involves violence, verbal and physical. If one is not happy where one is, one leaves, instead of telling someone else to leave. When the chief of the Plains Indians became too oppressive for his people, he woke up one morning to find that his teepee was the only one left on the plain. Everyone had quietly voted him in."

After a lot of problems with the transients at Morningstar, and harassment from the good burghers of Sonoma County who converged on the source of all that reputed sin, sex, and drugs, many of the community members retreated to Bill Wheeler's ranch not far away, which offered more room and more insulation from civilization.

Most of the groups that have formed since Morningstar began with the same idea about how a community should operate, and then made some compromises to protect against overcrowding, violence, and conflicts with neighbors and the local authorities (both police and health). Many of them have found that it is possible to work communally, to pool economic resources, to share meals and ceremonies, but only if everyone has a place of his own to retreat from the rest of the community. Sign-up lists for the essential tasks such as the gardening and the kitchen chores are fairly common. One group solved the problem of irresponsibility by assigning, on a rotating basis, the position of dictator-of-the-week.

Generally, there aren't any rules about who's allowed to stay and who's asked to leave. As one of the long-time residents of a Vermont commune put it, "We have a unanimous rule here. It's not like a democracy. A lot of people come here and want to stay, and it's almost always obvious the first few minutes or the first day whether they should. It's funny, it seems like there's some kind of force that repulses people when they don't belong here. Like there have been new people who are really groovy, whom everybody liked. But everyone said no. I mean everyone here represents a distinct facet of the family, and each one of us is a little different from anyone else."

In most cases the same consensual style operates when any decision has to be made. No action will be taken on a question until there is general agreement about it. And nearly all the larger communities have some sort of decision-making meeting in order to determine what the consensus is on important questions. Joined together in the first place by some common vision, most of the groups are able to resolve their problems in meetings and at the same time reinforce feelings of group unity. When this consensus-seeking process doesn't work, it often indicates a lack of unity, and a sign that part of the group should leave to form another community.

In their attempt to adopt an unstructured, leaderless style, most of the communes are by necessity small groups, much smaller than most of the nineteenth-century communities. Of all the hundreds of communes, only a few of the successful ones have more than thirty or forty members. As a consequence of face-to-face contact among all the members of the group, there is constant self-regulation which doesn't depend upon rigid rules or defined leaders. In this respect, too, the communes are faithful to the anarchist tradition. For Bakunin and Kropotkin, as for many other anarchists, the postrevolutionary society was to consist of small, intimate communities of primitive simplicity. The objection to this ideal has consistently been that it is impractical, that there is no way of translating it into a modern national society.[13]

In one of his essays, Alan Watts comments on the popularity of "Beat Zen" as a badge of disaffiliation. The great attraction of Zen, as opposed to Confucianism or the reigning varieties of Christianity, is that it is not completely absorbed in ethics. Rather than preaching or scolding, Zen in a sense cannot even be taught. It points beyond the categories of good and evil to a realm in which "anything goes." Above all else, Zen suggests the liberation of the mind from conventional thought, rather than rebellion against convention. But, as Watts observes, much of "Beat Zen" demonstrates a certain "underlying protestant lawlessness." It becomes a pretext for license, a justification for doing anything you want.[14]

Almost exactly the same thing could be said of the counter culture's use of the anarchist tradition. As "Beat Zen" has served as a rationalization for amorality and indiscriminate art, anarchism serves as an ideological sanction for extreme permissiveness and lawlessness. In the same way that Marcuse's writings are used as a touchstone by the young who have hardly penetrated his opaque prose, or that Zen phrases are thrown around by people who hardly understand that elusive tradition, so anarchism quickly degenerates into slogans that seriously distort the whole idea. As a body of ideas it is unusually vulnerable to what Theodore Roszak called "adolescentization."[15] Carried to its extreme, the ideology of do-your-own-thingism means that anyone who asks anyone else to do anything is on a "power trip." And the visions of the anarchist future sound suspiciously like campaign rhetoric. For example, the euphoria of Jerry Rubin's concluding paragraph in *Do It!*

> At community meetings all over the land, Bob Dylan will replace the National Anthem.
> There will be no more jails, courts, or police.
> The White House will become a crash pad for anybody without a place to stay in Washington.
> The world will become one big commune with free food and housing, everything shared.
> All watches and clocks will be destroyed.

> Barbers will go to rehabilitation camps where they will grow their hair long.
> There will be no such crime as "stealing" because everything will be free.
> The Pentagon will be replaced by an LSD experimental farm.
> There will be no more schools or churches because the entire world will become one church and school.
> People will farm in the morning, make music in the afternoon, and fuck whenever they want to.

As we know, no one has ever run a country—or a commune—on campaign rhetoric. Even if this is understood as a characteristic example of Jerry Rubin's rhetorical overkill, I think it's not an unfair caricature of the "adolescentization" of the anarchist tradition.

But, understood in a deeper sense, the anarchist tradition is valuable in much the same way that Zen is. Zen embodies a critique of the conventional scientific view of man and nature. Anarchism is a critique of cancerous growth and dysfunctional authority. For all the distortions of the anarchist tradition, the instincts of the young to revive its themes are very healthy indeed. Much of Western political thought can be read as a debate between the countervailing claims of freedom and order. The utopians have typically stressed order at the expense of freedom; the anarchists have done just the opposite. The utopian and the anarchist traditions can be understood as two possible directions for human development. The path that has been proposed by most of the utopians is to limit freedom and to create a uniformly ordered society. The anarchists have proposed that the only viable community is one in which people are self-regulating. Confronted by a society which in many ways reflects the spirit of the authoritarian utopias, it makes very good sense for the young to experiment with the alternative, small anarchist communities.[16]

Despite their differences about what the alternative society should look like, the problem is stated very similarly by two men rarely quoted in the same breath, B. F. Skinner and Paul Goodman. From *Walden Two:*

> I thought of the millions of young people who were at that moment choosing places in a social and economic structure in which they have no faith. What a discrepancy between ideal and actuality—between their good will toward men and the competitive struggle in which they must somehow find a place! Why should they not work out a world of their own?

And from Goodman's *Making Do,* as he considers the fate of the boy he loves:

> . . . for him—and not only for him—there was in our society NO EXIT. When he had asked his germane question, and the fifteen experts on the dais did not know an answer for him. But with ingenuity he had hit upon a painfully American answer, *Do It Yourself.* If there is no community for you, young man, young man, make it yourself.

And to an extent that neither Skinner nor Goodman could have anticipated, that is exactly what has happened.

6 : *Gathering Together*

> The gathering together of people in large communities
> is either a natural occurrence, as in the case of the
> family, or an artificial one, as in the case of the state.
> . . . Only collective moral force can unite the world.
> Such great times of unification will leave great achieve-
> ments behind them. . . . In the time of GATHERING
> TOGETHER, we should make no arbitrary choice of the
> way. There are secret forces at work, leading together
> those who belong together. We must yield to this
> attraction: then we will make no mistakes.
>
> *I Ching*—"Gathering Together"

The letters came from all over the country, from Lex-
ington, Kentucky, from Denver, from Willimantic, Connecticut. This one, written in an uncertain grammar-school
hand, came from a place called Muscoda, Wisconsin:

> Dear Brothers and Sisters,
>   I'm female, nineteen, and a college drop-out. Right
> now, I'm trying to keep from being swallowed by a
> monster—plastic, greedy American society. All of my
> friends are working to get through school, to start a
> job or get married and settle down. But the thought
> of following this pattern completely turns me off.
> Quitting school is a start, but what then? This is basi-

cally where my head's at now. The uptightness and the hustling of the city is not what I want, and for sure not what I need.

One of my brother's friends visited your commune a couple of months ago, and said you're really open and you accept everyone for what he is. None of the put-on which I have to live with here. Help me! I need to begin relating to new people who are into taking care of each other and the earth. I know nothing about farming, but I have to start somewhere, and I'm able and willing to learn. Please let me know whether I can come.

P.S. I don't mind getting rid of all my things, but I have a Labrador who's more like my child than a thing. He's friendly and hip. Can I bring him too?

Or another from a young couple in Highland Park, Illinois:

Hello—

Maybe we're not as much alone as I figured we were. I'm 25, working as an accountant. My wife, Beth, is 23, and a mother for our two boys, Matt and Jason.—There's nothing here that's sacred or loving, and we want out. We want a place for our children to grow up uninhibited and free to share the warmth of human relationships. We think we owe our kids— and ourselves—a new start. We know you don't have all the answers, but you have some of them. So that's it in a nutshell, my family and our dilemma. We'd like to become a part of your group. What more can I say? Please write and let us know if we will be welcome.

Peace and love to you all

The letters are addressed to places like Drop City, Clan Pax, the Heathcote Community, the Hog Farm, or the Georgeville Trading Post. Some of these groups are fairly easy to locate, well-known stops for the hip gypsies who happen to be passing by. Others are unnamed and unknown by all except those who have followed a vague set of directions given by the man at the gas station in the nearest town, who of course has heard about the freaks who live out beyond the McCurdys' farm, but doesn't approve.

Rural communes are scattered in clusters across the country in almost every region except the South and the Midwest. The first ones sprang up in California, north of San Francisco in Mendocino and Sonoma counties, and south off the coastal highway running down to Big Sur. Then a lot of the young people who were most serious about communal living left for northern New Mexico and southern Colorado to populate the area around Taos. By 1969, Vermont and the Hudson Valley near Woodstock were communal centers in the East. And in the last few years, new clusters have grown up in the Mount Shasta area in northern California, in Oregon around Eugene and Grant's Pass, and on the northwest coast around Seattle and Vancouver, British Columbia.

Despite some minor regional differences, such as the fact that craft-oriented communities are more common in New England than they are in the West, groups in different parts of the country are remarkably similar. One reason for this is that there is a great deal of migration from one commune to the next all across the country, creating a very efficient communications network about survival techniques, new groups, and "bad vibes." Even among the more stable communes, and the older ones—that is to say, any group that stays in the same place for two or three years—very few of the current residents are the same people who were there at the beginning.

The most important statistic about an eminently unstatistical movement is that every year since 1967 has brought an increasing number of communes. For every group that has been chased away or simply dissolved, several others have started up.

In the smallest groups, which typically include eight to ten people, membership is closed, publicity and visitors are actively discouraged, and the members' ages range from the late teens through late twenties. The larger groups include from twenty to forty members, most of whom are in their late teens or early twenties, and have a faster rate of turnover in membership.

Land is obtained in a number of different ways. In some cases, such as Lou Gottlieb's Morningstar Ranch, the founder buys the property and invites others to share it. In the Taos area, several hippie benefactors have purchased land and donated it for communal use. In other cases, the original members used their savings to purchase land, or monthly payments for land are scraped together. One other technique is to claim public land, some of which is still available through the government's Homestead Act.

But no matter how cheap the land, the limited income could not possibly sustain most of these groups for more than a few months if they didn't adopt a life style of voluntary primitivism. Needs are drastically reduced. The diet is fairly nutritious, although monotonous and low in protein. Clothing is secondhand or homemade. Whenever anything needs to be built or repaired, someone learns how to do it. And scavenging is raised to a high art. (If there were an award for resourcefulness in this category, the residents of Drop City, one of the first of the rural communes, would probably win it. They pioneered in making very respectable geodesic domes out of the tops of abandoned cars, and on one memorable night they dismantled an entire unused bridge.)

The most important characteristics of the communes don't yield to systematic observation. Facts and statistics could be marshaled to answer neatly defined sociological questions about life in the communes, group structures, consensual mechanisms, and leadership functions, not to mention the "how much," "how many," "when did you last" questions. But no list of characteristics says very much about what communal life feels like. I remember a few cautionary lines from a poem written "To Sociologists and Publicists of the Beat Generation":

> sorry to say
> you miss the point
> these things are lived
> not sociologized [1]

Each one of the hundreds of communes is at least a little different from any other, the result of the alchemy of particular individuals coming together. The task of trying to capture that uniqueness in words is a perilous one. One of the members of an Oregon commune gave me this advice: "Any family, any commune, is like a Rorschach test. What you see when you come here says more about who you are than what it is. Visitors come expecting to see free love, naked bodies, scruffy, idle, nonproductive hippies. And what they observe is some people embracing others, a few people walking around naked, and a lot of us just sitting around. But they completely miss what's really going on because they don't see what these things mean to us." Whether or not I have avoided these perils, I stand forewarned.

> This pictures a time when inferior people are pushing forward and about to crowd out the few remaining strong and superior men. . . . The upper trigram stands for the mountains, whose attribute is stillness. This suggests that one should submit to the bad time and remain quiet. . . . It is impossible to counteract these conditions of the time. Hence it is not cowardice but wisdom to submit and avoid action.
> —*I Ching*, "Splitting Apart"

Taos, New Mexico

In 1967, Haight-Ashbury was the place. Within a few years, the scene had shifted one thousand miles to the east, to Taos County, New Mexico. If the first hip settlers here had been searching only for a place that looked other-worldly, they couldn't have done better. Northern New Mexico is one of the few wilderness areas in this country which is even remotely inhabitable. When they first started to come here, the land was cheap. And since what they were looking for was a way to return to a life of primitive simplicity and, in some cases, to God, Taos must have seemed an ideal location. Everything back home had been easy: The only challenge were the bland predetermined demands of school and career. Here the parched land turns away all but the most determined farmers, and the winters sometimes reach temperatures of twenty below. Nature itself provides an initiation rite, a test of manhood which city life denies. For all its harsh-ness, nature also provides something else. Presiding over the whole valley are the rugged, supernatural Sangre de Cristo mountains.

Entering Taos, you can't miss the signs of a very un-natural turbulence in the air. Scrawled on the back of a billboard just outside of town is the message: HIPPIES– STAY OUT OR ELSE. Governor David Cargo hadn't used the word "hippie," but everyone knew what he meant when he commented, "It is fair to say that the appear-ance of substantial numbers of visitors in rural areas pos-sessing unsophisticated public services would strain New Mexican hospitality severely." It doesn't take more than a few minutes in Taos to notice that New Mexican hospi-tality has indeed been severely strained. Anyone with long hair is likely to be conspicuously ignored in the town's three luncheonettes; there are smashed windows, stories of late-night phone calls, arson, and threats of murder.

This seething intolerance is the result of radically different cultures trying to co-exist and not doing a very good job of it. The stable population of Taos County is about 75 percent Spanish-American, or Chicano. The rest of it consists of the "Anglos," most of whom cater to the tourists, and several thousand Taos Indians whose ancestral roots in the county reach back more than two thousand years. Most of the tension is between the local longhairs, perhaps a thousand of them, and the Chicanos. There could hardly be a more volatile combination. About a quarter of the Chicanos in Taos are unemployed, dependent on welfare and food stamps for their survival. Even those who are better off constitute part of an ethnic group that suffers the economic and social deprivation which are the lot of every minority group in America. Like other minorities, they learn to want what they will have little chance of attaining, the American middle-class way of life. Enter the city-bred hippies, many of whom come with money and college educations. And what do they do? They create their own communal society and ostentatiously deny the beliefs and the life style of the American middle class from which they are fleeing and to which the Chicanos are aspiring. The resentment is understandable, even if it seems that it needn't have escalated into violence.

On the outskirts of town, I stopped at the General Store, a communally operated hip information-center, grocery store, clinic, and underground Chamber of Commerce, all wrapped up in one glistening white building which contrasts with the reddish-brown adobe buildings throughout the rest of the town. Despite bullet holes in two of the plate-glass windows, it seemed to be a day of business as usual. There was an assortment of bearded or braless freaks and VW vans scattered around in front of the building. Operated by "The Family," which thinks of itself as a service commune, the General Store provides for the essential needs of the dozen or so communes that are located in the immediate area. At the store hippies can buy foods that are unavailable down the street at the supermarket, such as alfalfa seeds and fifty-pound bags of yellow cornmeal. The book rack includes an assortment of titles that are definitely not required reading for most local citizens, such things as *Stalking the Healthful Herbs, Being Your Own Wilderness Doctor, Letters from Sri Ramakrishna, Witches and Sorcerers,* and *Practical Astral Projections.* Next door is the free clinic, staffed by fourth-year medical students from the University of New Mexico. Although the health problems here haven't been as severe as they were in physically ravaged Haight-Ashbury during its heyday, the hip community has been afflicted with malnutrition and an assortment of infectious diseases. There are stories of a hepatitis wave that nearly wiped out several of the groups during the first years here.

There are other ways in which Taos has begun to resemble San Francisco during the Summer of Love. In fact, they've begun to call it Haight-Ashbury East. The biggest threat to the survival of the hip community here, even bigger than the threat of hostile Chicanos with .30-.30's in the middle of the night, is a massive hippie invasion. There have been rumors of a hundred thousand young people descending on the community during the summer. The locals would probably do the same thing that the townspeople did during the Woodstock Festival: declare the whole scene a disaster area at the first sign of the invading horde of long-haired barbarians. But even the hip community here is uptight about the prospect because, in a sense, they have more to lose. As one girl put it, "First we were chased out of the cities, then from the coast to more isolated areas like this one. Now we're being mobbed by the fugutives from the city insanity, and there's a whole new thing to worry about. Where can we go from here?"

On the bulletin board in the information center there was a message from The Family addressed to commune seekers:

> We are in the midst of a summer influx of people looking for communes in the Taos area. True, there are communes in the area, yet they are having a great deal of trouble surviving after a hard winter. Virtually all the communes in the area are now closed to newcomers. Recently the Hog Farm made a vital statement concerning this critical situation: "Any more people could easily kill us."
>
> Contrary to popular belief, hippies cannot come to Taos assured that welfare and food stamps will be handed to them by smiling Mexican-Americans. This is definitely *not* true, especially since recent legislation has made it nearly impossible to obtain them. The locals aren't smiling, especially at hippies. You may have heard stories of violence in Taos—believe them. This is not the place to come if you're not known here, have long hair, white skin, or black skin, or dress a little different. We recommend Utah for anyone looking for a place to start a commune.

And it's true. All the communes here, some of which have just begun to operate successfully after several years, are threatened by the hordes of curious visitors. The small, nameless families of ten to fifteen members living on a few acres of farmland are threatened least. But both the more organized groups with thirty or forty members such as New Buffalo, and the large unstructured "open land" groups where anyone can move in, set up a tent or sleep under the stars, and participate in the community as much or as little as he pleases, such as Morningstar East, run the risk of being strangled or simply split apart by too many newcomers.

I asked someone how to get to the commune where an old friend who had been living out here for several years was staying. After a cross-examination about my motives and my allegiances, he gave me the directions, north of town out toward Arroyo Hondo.

Leaving the main highway, you have to navigate about five miles of a neglected road, around potholes, over a small stream, a short wait for a small herd of sheep to move on, then down a sharp incline and into a broad valley circled by looming mountains. Thankfully, it was summer then and the road was dry, but how did anyone get in or out in the winter? In the distance, I saw a cluster of adobe huts, the carcasses of abandoned automobiles, a barefoot girl with braids and a faded ankle-length skirt, working in the fields. This must be it. But there was actually a barricade across the road, and a sign: NO CARS BEYOND THIS POINT. VISITORS ON THURSDAY AND SATURDAY ONLY. Obviously an attempt at immunity against Haight-Ashbury East. But how many people could find the place?

I parked where the tire ruts disappeared entirely and walked in the direction of the adobe building, through fields planted sporadically with what looked like beans and corn. I saw a tool shed, some enclosures for chickens, and several teepees scattered around the property, but only a few people. It was still pretty early in the morning and there wasn't much activity. The silence was interrupted only by occasional gusts of wind and someone playing guitar in the distance. Then two people, both probably in their late teens, erupted from the nearest building. The first to reach me was a plump, friendly looking girl. "Got any dope?" I didn't. "Any cigarettes?" I offered a pack to her, which she passed to the boy who was just behind her. I introduced myself. The boy, who was wearing a plain blue work shirt and one gold earring, said his name was Richard. He looked at me warily and asked me my sign. Capricorn.

"Far out. I'm a Libra, an air sign. I keep forgetting things."

We walked toward one of the rooms in the back of the compound. The whole building is remarkably well constructed. The only difference between it and the Indian pueblos is that here they have used glass in the windows. There's a propane-fueled water heater outside the room that must be the kitchen, but no overhead wires for electricity or a telephone. We knocked on one of the doors, and there was Allen, and a very pretty freckled girl he introduced as his old lady, Lakshmi (which, she later explained, is a Hindu symbol of prosperity and good fortune). With a Rutherford B. Hayes beard, a mod railroader cap, baggy overalls, and a gaping hole where two front teeth had been the last time I saw him, Allen was barely recognizable. I had been to college with him a few years before, but he looked as if he had been living in the austerity of New Mexico for half a century. He had been in decompression for a few years, and all the old nervous energy was gone, along with most of the ambitions. The old habits are out of place in Taos. The basketball hoop just outside his room seemed strangely inappropriate.

He invited me to stay and started talking about what he had done during the last three years. "The city was a really bad place for me. I was allergic to it, but it really took me a long time to admit it. So I went out to the coast for a while, bummed around, and finally ended up at Morningstar. You know, that was really a strange place. The conditions we lived under made us a really tight group. The neighbors got completely freaked out. All those people were coming in, and there was shit all over. It was a mess. So the courts got an injunction. The authorities said we didn't have enough flush toilets. Five gallons of water every time you flush the toilet! Can you imagine! That's the kind of thing that could really make you uptight about taking a dump.

"Then they said they'd arrest us for living in condemned structures. And finally it got so that it was illegal for anyone except Lou Gottlieb to set foot on the land. I mean, the police would come up five mornings a week, just before sunrise. You're lying in bed, and the man goes, 'Name, and date of birth,' and like if he catches your name and recognizes your face, you're busted. Keeps you on your toes. Finally, I got busted, and I was facing a choice. Either six months in jail or get out. So I packed my bags and got out.

"We heard about some free land out here and came, and it turned out to be a good place to be. For the first three months we made adobe bricks and tried to get our thing together before the snow came, and we just barely made it." Allen talked slower than he used to, but he still had the same way of looking straight at you when he talked. "For a while when we first came here, we were like a bunch of city kids at summer camp. Everyone was just amazed that they could actually make it in the country, that they could actually do it on their own, and make things grow. You should have seen us when the first crops started to come up.

"But you've really got to respect the land here. The message in a thousand ways is 'Take care of what you've got.' Because, man, if you fuck up the land, you fuck yourself up. It just isn't cool to rip off the land. You can't get away with it here. It isn't like California land. Here it takes a couple of generations to rejuvenate the land. For a while last year, we were using a tractor, but no more. It was expensive, and there were the fumes, and a couple of the new kids here used to get on it and take joy rides. So we got a horse and a mule, and the far-out thing is that the tractor didn't do the job any faster. And it's really hard to fuck up the land with a horse and a mule."

I asked about the Indians at the Taos Pueblo, and how anyone had learned to build houses out of adobe. Lakshmi, who had been sitting quietly next to Allen on a rug covering the dirt floor, answered. "The Indians . . . well, some of the people here really kiss their ass. But they're good people. They showed us how to build our houses, and how to plant the crops. We couldn't have made it without them. The Indians and the Chicanos, they're really on different trips. I mean, the Chicanos want all kinds of things, they really want to make it. But the Indians just want to live close to the land. They don't want very much, and they understand our trip. A couple of them heard we were into peyote. And they came out here and really showed us a few things. They know more about the cactus than anyone else. They come to visit pretty often, and they bring their drums and sing with us, and tell us what their songs mean. And we can really dig where they're at."

We talked for a while longer, then headed over to the kitchen for lunch, which consisted of dark bread, a salad made of tuna fish and some greens from the garden, and milk which someone had just brought from town. Most of the group, twenty or twenty-five people, was sitting or standing in the coolness of the kitchen as a welcome relief from the dry heat outside. Everyone was excitedly discussing the day's crisis. One of the local farmers had shot at Jezebel, a lean terrier, who had escaped damage and was contentedly sleeping in the corner of the kitchen while everyone talked about her.

By the time we finished, the temperature outside had reached at least ninety, and everyone was stripping off clothing in preparation for the afternoon's chores. The day's projects, which had begun this morning, were to cover an unused road with fresh compost which would later be plowed and planted, and to weed the pea patch. Although no one took work too seriously, and there were a good number of people who sat around after lunch or disappeared into their rooms, a fairly sizable work force collected out in the garden to help the one saw-backed nag with the plowing, the seeding, the irrigating, and the weeding. The crops include the bare necessities: potatos, onions, broccoli, corn, tomatoes, and some un-promising marijuana plants. As Allen explained it, "We try to put the land before the people here. Although this is liberated land that belongs to anyone as much as to the long-time residents here, the land really can't support more than thirty comfortably. So although we try to allow anyone to stay, no new building is encouraged because we want to maintain the present size. Any new people have to wait until a room is vacated before they can settle in."

After working for a while on the composting, I wandered over to where Freda, a gaunt, pigtailed, American-Gothic-looking girl, was determinedly weeding the garden. Inching along on her knees from one plant to the next, she started talking about her life here. "The reason for my being here is simply wanting to be a better person, to be in tune with myself and realizing that other people help me in that, searching for real values within yourself. A couple of years ago, I was really cynical, even through a whole series of acid trips, which is a pretty decadent reaction to an insane world. But after a while you get tired of your own void, so you start working constructively." She had grown up in Shaker Heights, left to attend college at Bennington, then was in New York working as a Kelly Girl. After a few years of what she described as "a pretty straight trip," Freda started to drop out, first as a part-time seamstress in the city, then to Vermont where she raised apples, and then to

Taos. "The thing that really disturbed me was the separation and distance people have with each other. You and I are one, after all," she said, looking up momentarily from her weeding. "And what we really have to learn is new ways to relate to each other. It's easy enough, one way or another, to survive, to have the things you have to have, but the difficult thing is to come together again as people. And communes are a way of doing that."

Among the more useful skills in the art of survival in Taos used to be the food-stamp game. A family of four could put down two dollars and get $26 worth of stamps in return. The only requirements were to convince the officials you were poor and to give them the right answers to a series of questions. But since it encouraged the hippie migration and became one of the important economic props of the whole nomadic culture, the policy was changed. "Actually, we feel a lot better now that we're no longer collecting welfare or food stamps," said Freda.

"That always was a hassle, giving them the right answer so that we could eat. This way, we either grow our own or starve, and that's funky. But we're still like a wart on the Establishment's ass. It's that kind of parasitic thing. We still really need the dollars that come in from outside. A month ago Larry's parents sent him money for the plane trip home to Georgia, and we've been living off that ever since, all of us. There's such an incredible surplus of wealth that we can make it on what little trickles our way. It's kind of like redirecting bad energy into good energy. But pretty soon, we'll be able to get along here without it."

A young couple had walked up the road, across the field, and over to where Allen and Iowa Tom were working with shovels and the wheelbarrow full of shit. The visitors offered a bottle of Red Mountain Burgundy and a lid of grass, asked if they could crash for the night, and Allen nodded that they could. I asked Freda, who was still creeping down the row of pea plants on her knees, whether they had many visitors and why the sign at the bottom of the road was there. "We'd like to be able to accept everyone who comes along," she answered, "and turn them on to our way of life here. But we can't. There are too many of them. It's a hassle because so few visitors understand that we're a family, we have to do some work, and a lot of them really bring in bad vibes. Like the bikers who stopped by here a week ago. We didn't want to put up that "No Visitors" sign, but we had to.

"About a month ago, we set aside a day for silent meditation and coming together because we had gone through a lot of bad things as a family. But this fellow comes drifting in with his transistor radio blasting rock and roll and absolutely shatters our silence. So we had to do something.

"But the real trip is with the other kinds of visitors. A week ago, we were all out here working in the afternoon, and up drives this baby-blue Cadillac with Texas plates and an 'I belong to the Silent Majority' sticker on the bumper, out on a little side trip to see the crazy freak farmers. The husband and wife in the front seat, two little kids in the back. It must have taken them hours to find the place, and I'm surprised that they could get their Cad over the stream at the bottom of the property, but here they were pretending that they had just lost their way en route to Las Vegas or something. They approached very slowly, the man and his wife doing this insane evasive thing, looking and not looking at the same time. The kids had their noses pressed to the windows, which were completely closed, of course. Got to be careful, it might be catching. Then one of the kids snuck the V-sign to Tom out in the fields here, and Tom flashed back a smile and held up two fingers in return, and it just made the kids' day. But what do you think the parents did? Did they stop and talk with us? They did not. They turned around in the courtyard and headed back where they came from. It's just too much. And they think *we*'re on some strange trip."

By about four o'clock, a light rain that we'd seen approaching through the mountains swept across the valley, and we ran back to the "family room," a round, below-ground-level room covered with a domed skylight ceiling on which the rain was spattering down. A fragile-looking boy who couldn't have been older than fourteen or fifteen, and who had been sitting around on his rucksack that morning looking forlorn, had just asked Ben whether he could stay for a few days. He was from Denver, out on the road for the first time, empty and searching. Ben told him he was sorry, but there weren't any rooms, and that there was a problem with the authorities with kids younger than sixteen. So the kid trudged back down the road in the rain, setting out for the next group up on the mesa, where he would ask the same question again and hope for a place where he'd be accepted.

I was standing at the door waiting for the rain to stop and listening to Peter, who was talking intently to a scared-looking girl about federal agents up in the hills, about an ominous plot to kill all the hippies by poisoning the water supply, about a new machine which the government was developing at Cal Tech to deaden people's cosmic consciousness. I had noticed a certain humorlessness among some of the members here, but this was something else. At first I was sure that he was kidding, that this was like ghost stories at midnight. But he wasn't. He was deadly serious, and his rap was an inspired concoction of mysticism, apocalyptic fervor, a smattering of technical phrases, and a heavy dose of paranoia. The girl sat there, guilelessly believing everything he said. Peter, who had a vacant, haunted face, had been booted out of school as a high-school sophomore and never returned. Recovering from months of heroin experimentation, he had spent his last three years looking for some hospitable place and had ended up here. Allen mentioned that he had drifted in one day several months ago and just stayed on, that he was preoccupied with these forebodings of things to come. I thought of Eric Hoffer's observation that the frustrated and the defeated were among the early adherents of all mass movements. Like Peter, they all grasp upon hatred and fear as the most accessible unifying agents. By decrying the present and its incurable evils, both real and imagined, Peter seemed to be softening his own feelings of frustration, failure, and isolation.

After a while the rain stopped, the sun came out again, and a dozen of us returned to the fields to finish the day's work. I walked out to the garden with a girl named Dawn who looked about twenty but said she was ageless. In a sense, she was right. Compared to its importance in the outside world where age is an index for career status and marital eligibility, where people learn to relate to each other in terms of age expectations, here one's age means very little. The importance of age has eroded in favor of a generous populism: The older people readily admit that they have as much to learn from the young as the young do from them. Chronological age is much less important here than experience and wisdom. The girls especially, like Dawn, seem to hover in an indeterminate twilight zone between their teens and middle age.

Dawn had arrived just a few days before, but she was thinking of moving on again. "This whole thing can really be a drag. There are lots of kids whose heads just aren't together. I'm hoping that things will work out better in California, because I just can't go back home." "Home" was Long Island, and a Jewish mother who Dawn said hadn't slept a night since she was eighteen. "There's nothing for me there. She connects the word 'moral' only with sex. But, I mean, I'm really stricter morally than she is. I'm willing to give up a lot of things in order to live the way I think I should be living. But she thinks I'm completely wigged out."

Dawn spent a few years at the University of Illinois, surrounded by sorority life and college football games. Then she left, worked on the McCarthy campaign, was radicalized, and almost immediately dropped out of politics. "I had just started to get into SDS and that kind of thing when I went to the Chicago Convention and was arrested at a sit-in. After the Convention I was convinced that there was no way to work for change within the system. So I kind of floundered around for a while.

"At first I wanted to make a new beginning as an artist, but that meant that I'd still have to participate in the competitiveness of that society. I'd have to sell my work and everything, you know. So it all came down to the realization that it wasn't possible to live in that society and not feel alienated. I went to a commune in Ann Arbor for a while, but they were into a political thing. And, I mean, radicals are so full of hate, just look at the screaming underground press. You have to put your own house in order before you can change anyone else's, and I don't think they've done that. . . . I like the simple life here," she said with a little shrug, "but I can't seem to get it together with the people."

Allen came over, finally finished with the composting, and Sunshine, a smiling four-year-old girl, came trailing uncertainly behind. Sunshine was one of the first of the commune babies. She had spent two years on the coast near Big Sur with her mother, Carol, before they came here. Although she still spent more time with her mother than with anyone else, child-raising was very much a shared responsibility, and Sunshine seemed to be happy about the whole situation. "Everyone takes his turn in a parental kind of role here," said Allen. "And all the kids are pretty precocious children because they have to keep up with this fantastic relationship. Sunshine's really a beautiful person, really uncorrupted, open and trusting."

Like most of the communal children, she is also unofficial. The entire process of state identification, registration, and certification is avoided. Birth certificates are scorned as the fatal beginning of an official assembly line which leads to compulsory public education, military conscription, social security, and taxation. The official system of licensed marriages is also rejected as a ludicrous government intrusion. Several couples here have remained monogamous as man and wife for several years, but have no intention of "making it official." For Sunshine, the problem will come in a few years when she's school age, and the group will have to decide whether to provide its own school or send her into the hostile, predominantly Chicano public schools. So far, none of the communes in the Taos area have organized their own schools.

"The test of this whole thing," said Allen, looking over to the handful of workers who were making their way back to the pueblo, "will be the next generation. All of us are still held back by a lot of the stupid things we learned before we came here. But the kids who grow up here, they're going to be really high people, absolutely out of sight."

Half an hour later we were all congregating in the kitchen, where Lakshmi and Nancy were working around the black iron wood-burning stove preparing a dish of brown rice and tomatoes. Hanging over the counter next to the stove was a sign-up list for kitchen chores and laundry, with the names of several of the girls listed opposite the jobs. "We don't believe in laying down too heavy a structure here," explained Allen. "So there is just this one list. Somehow everything else seems to get done sooner or later." It was strange to hear no one talking about Women's Lib. There's real work to be done, both by men and women. The heavy work, the building, maintaining the fires, most of the work in the fields—that's man's work. And the women do what most women were happy doing until dishwashers, laundromats, and day-care centers made housewives obsolete: They take care of most of the cooking, the sewing, and the laundry, help with the crops, and keep an eye on the children. Veblen dismissed the housewife's role as "an occupation of ceremonial futility," but out here where everyone is more dependent on everyone else than back where they all came from, where women aren't expected to raise children in isolation from all other adults except a part-time father, things are different. It's a pretty traditional way of handling what needs to be done, but no one seems to be complaining or attempting to change it.

It was almost eight o'clock when dinner was ready, and Nancy went outside to ring the bell for the few family members who hadn't already gathered in the kitchen around the rough homemade table. Everyone was quiet for a minute, standing around the large table holding hands. Tom bowed his head and began the simple blessing: "Dear Heavenly Father. Thank You for the day here, the warmth of the sun, and our brotherhood here together. May we always be thankful for the good food which comes from the land. May we grow together here with your help. Amen."

For a few minutes, as everyone started eating, the silence was broken only by the barking of a dog outside and the clinking of metal cups. I began to feel like a sailor becalmed at sea. The pace of things was so slow that it felt as if nothing was happening. Iowa Tom said something about the crops coming up well this season, and the plump girl who had met me when I first arrived commented about the solstice festival planned for the next week. But mainly there was just silence and the fading light outside. I felt the urge to talk, to fill up the silence which apparently bothered no one else. And I remembered something that Alan Watts wrote: "Excessive verbal communication is really the characteristic disease of the West." This must be what he meant. It was what Allen had mentioned that morning when he spoke about "the city trip": "When people get here, they've just come from the city, and like they expect everybody to be madly running about, and all sorts of things constantly happening. So you arrive here, and you're still on that same kind of nervous trip. The first couple of days, or even the first month or so, is like decompression, and then you begin to get into the rhythm of nature and this kind of life."

After dinner, Allen, Lakshmi, and half a dozen others were sitting around a fire built in one of the teepees. The couple who had arrived that afternoon sat there together, she softly playing on a flute, he tapping his fingers on a homemade drum. Lakshmi was sitting all wrapped up in an Indian blanket to protect her from the coolness outside, thinking back to the last time she had been East, at Sunrise Hill, one of the early communes in New England. "I'm not a mystical person, but I had a three-day mystical experience without drugs at Sunrise Hill. I felt that the environment was so warm and loving that there needn't be any boundaries between me and others, no need to cover or hide. It was such intense living all the time. But of course it ended. One of the other members ended it by really hurting me. But that experience made me resolve that I had to live that way from then on. Despite everything, the quality of relationship was so good that I realized that any other kind is tinny. My definition of a commune is not just sharing a house and kitchen because it's cheaper. It's sharing work, a common purse, and a future life together that we're all involved in.

"Ordinary life is so incredibly fragmented, living in an apartment, seeing your friends once or twice a week, and then only when they're at their best behavior, sitting at coffee, exchanging lives as comparisons of 'Well, what have you been doing lately?,' which is so different from what we're into here, living really close to each other."

Allen sat watching the smoke from the fire pass through the flap in the top of the teepee, nodded, and quietly agreed, "Right on."

> What is required is that we unite with others, in order that we may complement and aid one another through holding together. . . . Late-comers must suffer the consequences, for in holding together the question of the right time is also important. . . . Common experiences strengthen these ties, and he who comes too late to share in these basic experiences must suffer for it if, as a straggler, he finds the door locked.
> —*I Ching,* "Holding Together"

Grant's Pass, Oregon

Things are cooler, greener, and friendlier in Oregon. There are signs of new hip settlements throughout the southwestern part of the state. In restaurant windows in Cave Junction, the message that CUSTOMERS MUST WEAR SHOES is posted, and there is a thriving health-food store in Grant's Pass. So far, there isn't much hostility between the hippies and the local residents.

I pulled off the highway at one of those tourist centers that dispense information about campgrounds, state parks, and local motels, and the girl at the desk not only gave me directions to the commune I was looking for, but said she knew most of the members and visited there regularly.

I picked up one of the group members who was hitch-hiking seven miles from the main road to the communal land up in the hills, and he confirmed my impression of friendly co-existence. "They aren't hip in town," he said, "but they're into our trip. When we first came out here two years ago, none of us knew what we were doing, so we asked the local people. They were a little suspicious at first, but when they saw that we were serious about putting in buildings and crops, they helped us, and made us feel welcome."

We traveled for several miles before turning onto another, narrower road. I noticed that nailed to the trees there were signs marked with arrows and the word FIRE. Sitting next to me as we bounced along, Jerry explained what had happened. "Some people came up to visit us a couple of days ago. They didn't know anything about living in the woods, especially in the middle of the summer when this whole place is like a tinderbox. One evening they started a campfire up in the woods, and before they knew what was happening it was a huge fire. It wouldn't have taken long for our whole place, all two hundred acres of it, to go up in flames, but the state Fire Rangers got here pretty quickly, following these signs. And a lot of the local people came out to fight the fire with us. So we got it under control after a while, and we really learned a thing or two from it. I mean, it really pulled us together as a group. That evening when we gathered and held hands before dinner we really had a heavy Om. The lesson of that fire was: Don't store up your treasures here, because this is what'll happen if you do."

We pulled over to the side of the road to let one of the state Forest Rangers' trucks pass. The Rangers, who had returned to pick up some of their tools and to check to see that none of the stumps were burning, smiled and waved, then pulled past and disappeared in a trail of dust.

As for many of the more successful communes, one of

the chief attractions of this location is that it is so hard to reach. "If we didn't have this deeply rutted road," Jerry remarked, "we'd be deluged. It really sets us back in the nineteenth century. But, after all, we're more interested in discovering the past than the future." We made one final turn, past a small marker with a peace sign on it, then down a path which was framed on both sides with lush green plants and trees.

We parked just beyond a small, neatly planted garden and went on foot in the direction of the largest building, the lodge. The densely wooded property is dotted with tents, teepees, and lean-tos made with whatever materials are available, what they call "biodegradable architecture." There are no electricity and no telephones, although during the week that I stayed there, I noticed that one of the popular diversions, especially among the newer members, was frequent trips to the pay phone at the nearest gas station five miles away. The most conspicuous concession to the demands of permanency is the hexagonal lodge built of logs, which serves as kitchen, the group's common room, and sleeping area for about twenty people, which is half the summertime population. In the winter almost everyone sleeps in this one building. But now sleeping bags and an assortment of jerry-built structures were scattered all over. Everything reflected the belief that it's far more dangerous to care too much about things than to disregard them.

The membership is slightly older than most of the rural communes, but the assortment of backgrounds that people come from is typical. Several members came from San Francisco or Berkeley, where they were street people, doing nothing in particular. One was a musician, another a carpenter, a third a doctor. There were several master's degrees. Susan, one of the long-time members, had a degree from Swarthmore, and her husband, Jeffrey, was doing computer-programing. But for many people here, education was simply irrelevant, so they dropped out. As Diane, a tall, cheerful, strawberry blond who had been an art major in college, put it, "Well, I started in college, but it got to the point where even if I got a degree, there was nothing that I would have wanted to do with it, so I left."

She was married with two kids and living in the suburbs, but she started to grow away from her husband. "I started smoking, and took acid a few times, and I began to look at things differently. Like when I started smoking, I stopped dusting. It just didn't make any sense spending all that time dusting all those things. Then I took acid, and when I put that little pill in my head all of a sudden I understood a lot of things for the first time. I knew what was important, the love and the sharing, and these other things just weren't important at all. But my husband, he still wanted things of his own, and he didn't want to open up the house to others, so we split and I came here."

The residents here have avoided some of the problems of the Taos community by settling farther north, but there are different problems, like the long winters. Although some of the members leave almost every winter, travel south, or simply scatter until spring, about a dozen people stay all year round. Out beyond the parking area there was a huge pile of firewood which would be used up by next March. And in the storage shed, there were the beginnings of next winter's food supply: dried fruit, some canned goods, and herbs.

But, in general, no one seemed very much concerned about stocking up on provisions for the winter, or planning ahead in any respect. One of the things that people often say here, and it seems to be a habit of mind as well as a figure of speech, is, "It will be manifest." The simple faith that problems will take care of themselves is demonstrated daily in dozens of ways. I asked Susan where

the money came from to feed forty people a day, to buy
the provisions that weren't grown here. "It's really hard
to give an answer to that," she said, "because the money
just comes. Oh, there are a lot of people who have
dropped out who are pretty affluent, and that's where we
get part of what we need. But sometimes it'll be two
hours before mealtime, and no one on this whole property
will have any money, and there will be forty people to
feed. And yet it comes. Somehow there's always enough,
and I can't ever remember a 'No Meal' here. Every
month we have to pay a hundred dollars for the land and
we have to buy a lot of the food, but it comes. Like a
couple of weeks ago, we found two hundred-dollar bills
in the can in the kitchen."

Susan and her husband Jeffrey had been Quakers active in civil-rights work. They participated in a civil-rights
protest in Los Angeles several years ago in which the
police started clubbing people as a "riot control" technique. As Susan now explained, "That was what got us
started. All those innocent people getting clubbed. Then
we began to understand that all those protests just
weren't going to do anything except breed hate."

In the summer, people have as much privacy as they
want since they can spread out over the whole two-hun-
dred-acre property. But in the winter, said Cecil, his
goatee twitching when he talked, it could be a problem.
"Sometimes the lodge is like a popcorn popper. Some
people will be arguing in one of the cubicles, in the next
a couple will be making love, in the next someone will
be meditating, and in another someone's reading stories
to the children—all those things going on at once. But
the whole trick to living here is to be flexible with what's
going on, the whole lesson is one of tolerance. There are
some people who are operating on higher levels than
others, but you try to understand that. Like we really get
down on each other here. We assume that we know each

other intimately because we are one another. It's really hard to keep relating that way every day when we're constantly together—bathing together, eating together, working together. We've found that every one of us needs a little room for himself, unlike a lot of the early communes which were pressure cookers because everyone was physically on top of everyone else all the time. And after a while, that kind of thing just has to blow up."

The policy about visitors is looser here than it is in Taos, in part because the property is more remote. As Cecil explained, "The Lord is generous here, so in the summer there's no problem. Some people feel that every time visitors come we have to put out all this energy answering questions and showing people around. But that's one of the things we're doing, letting people know that there are other ways of living."

There is a steady stream of migrant hippies coming and going. Some of them stay for a night or a few days. Others, if they are accepted by the members, stay indefinitely. One day the visitors included Daniel, a well-known figure in these parts, looking for all the world like an itinerant preacher slightly updated. He approached, looked directly into my eyes for about a minute with an embarrassing intensity, then was into his gentle rap, leaping from the demonic to the ecstatic: "This whole generation, all these people born since 1943, they've been exposed to entirely new vibes from the universe, creating an entirely new species." For a moment he seemed lost in his thoughts, rocking back and forth in a plain brown garment which looked like a monk's habit. ". . . You see, brother, the difference between the Piscean and the Aquarian age, it's like this: In the Piscean, Christ appeared as one man, and it was told that in the next age, every man would see himself as Christ. Well, that's happened, brother, and it's our task not just to learn about Christ, but to live the life that Christ lived. . . . But the end is near. It really is. This whole trip's about to end, and like people who know aren't planning anything after 1976 or 1977. . . ." Daniel was accepted as a "really high" person, a holy man, and most of the members respected his message even if they weren't so intensely religious themselves.

In a way that isn't very obvious almost everyone here is religious, although hardly in a Sunday-school sense. Cecil tried to explain it one afternoon: "I think all of us have had the Experience. It's from whatever that substance was that we all took back in 1965. One way or another, this whole thing revolves around LSD-25. You take that stuff, and it takes you all the way back, cell for cell, vibration for vibration, back to the common denominator, that one seed which we all came from. Everyone shares that. But you can't define it, and it's kind of a game to talk about it, because words just aren't very useful at all in describing it. But everyone knows what everyone else saw. And after that experience you just don't want to live the way you used to. It doesn't make any sense. That's why this whole place is such a weird conglomeration of things. I mean, it isn't a gradual kind of growth. This whole trip started when all of a sudden somebody put this thing into your hand that flashed you into the core of the universe. And a few hours later, there you are again, you're more or less the same person, but you have to figure out some way of living which makes sense in terms of that experience you had."

Cecil had been an actor before he came, and he still had a way of pausing for effect. "You see, LSD is like a back brain. Our normal working consciousness is like a front brain. Front brain doesn't know much about back brain being there. There's your front brain, your intellect, rapping on, talking about this, that, and the other thing, knowing facts, having taste and sophistication. But in the back of your brain there's that whole evolutionary core that you're cut off from. But all of a sudden it's reversed on you. You take that little pill, and all of a sudden front brain understands that the whole thing was a huge perceptual error."

There are drugs here, but not many "drug problems." Marijuana is used about the same way that coffee is taken elsewhere. And although a few people have completely stopped taking acid, for most it's still the most important sacramental drug. "I don't think anyone here's on co-caine, speed, or heroin," said Ariel, a veteran of two years in the East Village who was busily doing her wash on an old-fashioned washboard. "When anyone brings grass or acid, we all share it and everyone gets stoned. But most of the people here are naturally pretty high anyway."

As in most of the other rural hip settlements, the daily routine here is a simple one. In the morning, the big gong hanging from the tree by the lodge is rung, and members straggle in from all parts of the property for coffee and a simple breakfast. During the day there is work to be done: planting, weeding, harvesting in the garden, splitting logs, or fishing. Frequently a few members will go out to work at day labor such as crop picking. And there's a series of projects to work on, such as the new septic tank which had to be installed. There is a lot of time, though, for sitting around, talking, and walking in the sun. In the evening, there's the meal together, then music on the platform back in the woods, and quiet hours after dark for talking or reading by the kerosene lamps. The diversions include trips into Grant's Pass to the laundro-mat, and maybe a stop on the way back for ice cream, candy bars, or pizza as a change from a fairly monoto-nous diet. But, in general, especially among the members who have been here longest, there's little interest in the outside world, including radical politics. "We have a pretty good idea what's going on out there," said Diane, "and we don't want any part of it."

The one newspaper that somehow found its way to the

main table in the lodge during the week I was there was viewed as a curiosity rather than a necessary link with the world outside. Everyone here would heartily agree with what Thoreau wrote from his retreat at Walden Pond: "I have no time to read newspapers. If you chance to live and move and have your being in that thin stratum in which the events which make the newspapers transpire —thinner than the paper on which it is printed—then these things will fill the world for you. But if you soar above or dive below that plane, you cannot remember nor be reminded of them."

The visitors provide some variety to the daily routine. One of them, a short, blond girl who had been there for a few days, looked as if she had just traded in her pom-poms and her cheerleader's skirt for a peasant dress and leather thongs, but hadn't quite made the mental adjustment yet. She kept approaching family members and running through her one-line statement of faith. "I really dig the silence, the good air, and the simple food. . . ." But the line was delivered in a style which would have been appropriate if she were eagerly trying to gain membership in a college sorority.

One afternoon the parents of one of the newer members, a girl from New Orleans who had dropped out of college in Los Angeles and come here to live, drove up in a dusty car. They had flown from Louisiana to San Francisco, rented a car, and arrived unannounced to retrieve their prodigal daughter. From the looks on their faces as they approached the lodge, everything confirmed their worst suspicions. One of the girls was standing under the shower out in back of the lodge. It wouldn't have occurred to her to be self-conscious about the fact that she was standing there naked, except that the father was glancing about uneasily while Mother warily approached someone to ask about her daughter's whereabouts. They couldn't have looked more distraught if they'd just seen the Four Horsemen, but rather than war, famine, pestilence and death, they would have renamed them dirt, sex, drugs, and disorder. Mother and daughter fought to a draw: Patty would spend a few days with them in San Francisco discussing her return to college if they'd spend a few days here trying to understand why she had come. But of course the parents insisted on taking a room at the Holiday Inn fifteen miles away.

One of the new arrivals sauntered in wearing a big cowboy hat and managed within a few hours to get into arguments with almost everyone on the property. The visitor, promptly dubbed "Pistol," then wandered down to the swimming hole where he started to kill snakes with a club. With a crooked smile he boasted that this was something that he was really good at. Then he began to ogle all the naked female bodies sunning or swimming in the creek. The girls felt so uncomfortable in his presence that a small posse of males was organized to tell "Pistol" he'd better get out by sundown. He did.

I was talking with Cecil and Diane in their tarpaper lean-to a few days later, discussing "Pistol" and his sexual overtures. "That's a pretty normal trip for people who have just dropped out," said Cecil. "His parents probably scheduled twice-a-week sex for twenty years, and he thinks that as soon as gets away from that whole thing he should become a committed voluptuary. We've had some problems with that one. Some of the people who come here just want to make it with everyone all the time. But, after a while, everyone gets into his thing. Most people are kind of coupled off, and a few are doing a celibate thing. It works itself out." He sat there for a moment, pulling on his goatee, then looked up again. "But one of the best things that happens here is that you can put your arm around someone without implying the sexual thing."

The lean-to was furnished with most of the earthly

possessions that Cecil and Diane really cared about: a guitar, a few books, a lantern, a sleeping bag. Diane sat there intently shredding a long blade of grass that she had plucked from the ground, and Cecil continued: "Sometimes you have to go a long way out of your way in order to go a short way correctly. I mean, most of what we're doing here should be magnificently obvious. Like the trip with things. Now there's a constant master-slave relationship: Do I own my things or do they own me? What kind of nonsense do I have to go through in order to have my fifty-thousand-dollar house, my Stingray with dual carbs, and my eighty-watt fifteen-channel stereo set? It's pretty obvious that it's hard to have all those things and not get attached to them. So what we're doing here is to get back to something really simple: The fewer things you have, the easier it's going to be to figure out what's important.

"And we handle the leadership thing the same way, by getting back to something really simple and obvious. No one here has any more weight than anyone else, but we all know that some of us can do certain things better than others. Ariel knows more about the crops, about the growing seasons, and that kind of thing than any of the rest of us, so she's kind of the leader in that area. Ron knows how to fix things. Bob knows how to build things. And Liza, who doesn't know how to do anything or make anything, her specialty is being kind of a Supermother here. I mean, when things really get tough and people start to get on one another's nerves, she kind of keeps us together. . . . That's why we have to grow slowly here, because it's like a mosaic. Everyone has his own kind of strength and his own weakness to overcome. But we've come to a point where we work pretty well as a group. And if a bunch of freaks like us who don't know anything about anything can get together and be a family in the woods, then anybody can do it."

Late one evening after most of the other members of the family had gone to bed, Susan was sitting at the table in the lodge, sewing a patch on a battered pair of blue-jeans by the light of a kerosene lamp. She showed me something she had just written, a reply to a letter the group had received, which was really a credo for communal living:

> From the first seed of life, we are brothers and sisters. Our bodies are from the same womb. Here we are one with the Earth and know her as our Mother, and through her our heavenly Father.
>
> You can do it! Getting out of the city isn't hard, only the concrete is. Get it together with a few of your friends. Have like intent. Buy land. Don't rent. Money manifests. Trust. Go live in a tent, make a tipi, a lean-to, plant a garden. Create a center. Come together!
>
> Have patience. Have faith. Growing close takes time. These are the lessons learned: Do it yourself. Become self-reliant. Make a family, a tribe. Keep it tidy. Flexibility is vital to organic growth. Numbers are cumbersome.
>
> Many are curious, many truly seeking. Turn them on to turn within. Keep your heart open. Provide rest for the weary, a meal for the hungry, and food for the nourishment of the soul. Plant a seed. Don't be fainthearted. Ask those who stay too long to move on and let the seed take root. From one come many. Ask them to go forth rejoicing.
>
> If a brother stands in the dark, be the light that he may see. Be strong. Slay the ego. Be humble. Give thanks to our Father. Heaven and earth are here and now, ours to inherit. Praise the Lord! Hallelujah! Hare Krishna!
>
> > Peace and Love,
> > Brothers and Sisters

7 : *Individualism and Collectivism*

> Now the slave is free; now all the stubborn, hostile
> barriers, which necessity, caprice or shameless fashion
> have erected between man and man, are broken down.
> Now, with the gospel of universal harmony, each one
> feels himself not only united, reconciled, blended
> with his neighbor, but as one with him.
>
> —Nietzsche

Perhaps the only mental habit that the dissenting young
and their elders have in common anymore is nostalgia.
The faster a hyperactive technology carries us into an
uncertain future, the more we look for our fashions and
our entertainment to the quaintly familiar past, to
"Golden Oldies," Ruby Keeler, and *No, No, Nanette.*
Many of the themes of the counter culture reflect this
same nostalgia. They are attempts not to discover the
future but to recover the past, to return to a preindustrial
world which was simpler and more stable than our own.

In Peter Laslett's words, this is "the world we have
lost." It was hardly idyllic but, as Laslett points out, it
provided a kind of security unknown to modern man.
"Time was, and it was all time up to 200 years ago, when
the whole of life went forward in the family, in a circle of
loved, familiar faces, known and fondled objects, all to

human size. That time has gone forever. It makes us very different from our ancestors." [1]

The awareness of "the world we have lost" has been one of the chief preoccupations of artists and intellectuals since the nineteenth century. In literature, religious thought, and psychiatric writings, the vocabulary of estrangement, anxiety, uprootedness, and insecurity is the legacy of the twin facts of industrialization and individualism. Nowhere has this preoccupation been stronger than among social theorists trying to assess the dislocations that followed the collapse of medieval society. Emile Durkheim, the French sociologist, found that suicide and insanity occurred most often in those parts of society where moral and social individualism were greatest, where the individual had few close bonds to the group. Georg Simmel commented on the depersonalizing influence of money as a means of exchange. Perhaps the most influential statement on the breakdown of traditional community was written by Ferdinand Tönnies, who contrasted *Gemeinschaft,* the integral community of traditional society in which there was a fusion of feeling, thought, commitment, and tradition, with *Gesellschaft,* rationally ordered society in which most social contracts are merely functional relationships. Yet despite this chorus of doubt about the trajectory of modern society and the premonition that an increasingly rationalized society in which men are cut off from communal structures might be unlivable, there has been no effective counterweight to industrialization and individualism.

One of the themes of the counter culture is rebellion against all the atomistic tendencies of modern society, a full-scale attack on the received notions of how people relate to one another, and an attempt to recover "the world we have lost." Since the Free Speech Movement at Berkeley in 1964, demands for an end to the war, for student power, and for liberation of the oppressed have been accompanied by a distinctly different sort of demand—for psychic liberation and new human bonds. The students who carried signs that read Do Not Fold, Spindle, or Mutilate and demanded a "campus community" were expressing a diffuse feeling of estrangement that extended far beyond the Berkeley campus. Being "processed" by the university's remote bureaucracy was symptomatic of the depersonalization of the whole society.

Since 1964, this concern for psychic liberation, for storming the barricades that have been erected between men, has become one of the most persistent themes of the revolt. In its production of *Paradise Now,* the Living Theater announced its intention to "envelop the audience in churchly communion." At the Chicago trial, Allen Ginsberg stated that the only way this nation could save itself was through "an infusion of feeling, of tenderness, of fearlessness, of spirituality, of natural delight in each other's bodies." The range of available techniques for getting back in touch, both with ourselves and others, now extends from once-a-week encounter sessions to ritual nakedness. Nakedness—whether that of the cast of the Living Theater stripped for a performance of *Paradise Now* or the casual nudity of the communes—symbolizes the stripping away of the artifices of civilization, an attempt to get back to the condition of "natural man," unencumbered by guilt and inhibitions.

The lexicon of the communal movement reflects a very conscious desire to return to the integral community of preindustrial society. The word "tribe" has been revived, as Gary Snyder explains, "because it suggests the type of new society now emerging within the industrial nations. In America of course the word has associations with the American Indians, which we like. The new subculture is in fact more similar to that ancient and successful tribe, the European Gypsies—a group without nation or territory which maintains its own values, its language and religion, no matter what country it may be in. . . . Tribe proposes personal responsibilities rather than abstract centralized government." [2]

In the tradition of the utopian socialists, the counter culture joins what Martin Buber called "the most intimate of all resistances—resistance to mass or collective loneliness." [3] The tribal ethic, encounter groups, the slogans of "Love" and "Brotherhood," the joy taken from massive pilgrimages to Woodstock or the Isle of Wight, all counterpose a collective ideal to the dominant current of individualism. There is no better statement of the ideal than Nietzsche's description of Dionysian man, for whom "the union between man and man is affirmed. . . . Each one feels himself not only united, reconciled, blended with his neighbor, but as one with him; he feels as if the veil of Maya had been torn aside and were now merely fluttering before the mysterious primordial unity." [4]

The danger of any form of nostalgia is that it is so simple to imagine a past which never existed. It is seductively easy to assume that, until the beginning of the industrial age, community universally meant that one was always close to the warm bosom of cherished friends and welcome traditions. This is what Morton Grodzins called "the Gemeinschaft Grouse," the lament that industrialization caused the total dissolution of community and the deterioration of life, leaving in its wake only alienation.[5] Expressions of isolation and loneliness *are* typical of the industrial age, but so is another quite different theme. One of the central ideas that took hold in the seventeenth and eighteenth centuries and was passed on in diluted form to the nineteenth and twentieth centuries was that of individualism. The dominant objectives were those of release from the straitjacket of custom and tradition, from the constant surveillance of the traditional community. Until fairly recently, American literature was sprinkled with Carol Kennicotts, all trying to escape the tyranny of small towns like Gopher Prairie, Minnesota. For the Carol Kennicotts of the world, this nostalgia for the greater security of small towns or tribal cultures, as well as the Dionysian ideal of "primordial unity," would have seemed utter nonsense.

Several years ago in his widely acclaimed book, *The Secular City*, Harvey Cox answered the critics of urban life and, by implication, the critics of the impersonality of the whole of modern industrial society.[6] Rather than bemoaning the characteristically urban trait of smashing tradition and accelerating mobility from one place to another, thereby encouraging anonymity, Cox's book is a celebration of the freedoms of urban life. He argues that modern man encounters many more people in the course of his daily life than did his ancestor in traditional society; he *has* to keep some of them at a distance in order to preserve time and energy for his more meaningful relationships. Especially for urban man, Cox says, community does not consist of intimacy based on kinship or propinquity, but is rather a chosen set of friends who share common loyalties and interests. *The Secular City* performs the useful task of reminding us not to resort to facile romanticism about "the world we have lost." But what is missing from the discussion is a recognition of the erosion of communal structures in modern society.

For all its nostalgia, I think that the insistence on new communal bonds in the counter culture is also something else, a response to a very real problem in American society. The social historian Philippe Ariès has pointed out how drastically the meaning of the family and the concept of the individual have changed during the last four centuries, and in doing so he helps us to understand how peculiar some of our basic assumptions about social life really are. Studying the iconography of the ages since

the sixteenth century—the images of society preserved
in works of art such as paintings or engravings—Ariès
discovered something that was too commonplace to merit
the attention of contemporary writers. In most ages social
evolution, changing ideas about the meaning of everyday
life, is much too slow to be "newsworthy." And yet, as
Ariès found, enormous changes took place within a few
hundred years. Art in the sixteenth century was rarely
devoted to family scenes. Like Bruegel's memorable scene
at a peasant wedding, it depicted the crowd, "not the
massive, anonymous crowd of our overpopulated cities,"
as Ariès observes, "but the assembly of neighbors, women
and children, numerous but not unknown to one another." Life was lived in public, and there was neither
time nor place for solitude or privacy.

Even the seventeenth-century family, as Ariès points
out, was distinguished from the modern family by the
"enormous mass of sociability which it retained." Houses
were designed for communal living, and there was a constant flow of visitors at all hours. Privacy existed hardly
at all even within the house: People ate, slept, danced,
worked, and received visitors in the same room.

But in the eighteenth century something began to happen that we can see very clearly in our own time, the
triumph of the modern family over other types of human
relationships. "The family began to hold society at a distance, to push it back beyond a steadily extending zone of
private life. . . . The old code of manners was an art of
living in public and together. The new code of manners
emphasized the need to respect the privacy of others."
There was a new concern for the individual, for privacy
and comfort, for children and domestic matters. "Starting
in the eighteenth century, people began defending themselves against a society whose constant intercourse had
hitherto been the source of education, reputation, and
wealth. . . . Everywhere the family reinforced private life

at the expense of neighborly relationships, friendships and traditional contacts. The history of modern manners can be reduced in part to this long effort to break away from others, to escape from a society whose pressure had become unbearable." As Ariès says, he was tempted to conclude that "sociability and the concept of the family were incompatible, and could develop only at each other's expense." [7]

In the Middle Ages, Jacob Burckhardt wrote, "man was conscious of himself only as a member of a race, people, party, family, or corporation—only through some general category." [8] Since then, two huge facts have shaped the meaning of everyday life: the reality of the separate, autonomous individual, and the growing importance of the conjugal family at the expense of other forms of association. In recent decades we can see the result of this process which, according to Ariès, began in the eighteenth century: Family life has become a very private affair. Increasingly, in modern society, a man's "community" is his conjugal family.[9]

The process is epitomized in suburban living, whose chief virtue is that it offers escape from unbearable pressures. To quote from an ad selected almost at random from the real-estate pages of the *New York Times:* "Through these gates you will find the Impossible Dream! —Full Acre Homesites afford the utmost security, privacy, and seclusion from today's hectic tension and turmoil. . . ." Compared to the tenor of suburbia, even the respectable middle-class neighborhoods in most cities as recently as two generations ago were hotbeds of heterogeneity. Suburban neighborhoods are neatly defined homogeneous zones designed to protect their residents against the intrusions of the unfamiliar and the unexpected. More important than this homogeneity is the kind of communal life that suburbia offers. Affluence weakens the need for interdependency.

But the strangest aspect of modern suburban life to a visitor from the sixteenth or seventeenth century would be the extreme narrowing of the range of places where real human contact takes place. Ariès comments on the importance in the Middle Ages of tournaments, public dancing, festivals, parlor games, and games of skill as means of participation for everyone in the community. In France, the liveliness of café life is evidence of the fact that a good deal of one's social life there still takes place in public. One of the obvious differences between the meaning of a neighborhood in American suburban communities and its meaning in any of the remaining ethnic ghettos is that in suburbia there are so few places outside the home where people congregate. The social clubs, pool halls, and local bars which are still important places for amusement and social contact in many working-class neighborhoods have no equivalent in suburban middle-class neighborhoods. Most entertainment in the suburbs takes place in the privacy of the home, by invitation only. Rather than the diversity of social contacts that people have typically found in the wider arena of the village or the neighborhood, the suburban expectation is that almost all of one's most important social and emotional needs can be satisfied by the immediate family.

This is not to argue that in the wake of the ascendant nuclear family there are no other associations. Tocqueville astutely observed more than a hundred years ago the American penchant for organizing groups to accomplish everything from promoting the public safety to guarding its morality, and there is still a considerable array of such groups. But these organizations are formed to serve particular ends, and they hardly provide for emotional needs. It is the burden of the family to provide the affection, the security, and the feeling of "belonging" which are lacking in the rest of the society.

We bring these exaggerated needs to the family at a

time when it is particularly ill-equipped to meet them. Paradoxically, while the family has become increasingly fortified against the rest of society, it has lost many of the functions which gave it the vitality it once had. One of the important reasons why the extended family of an earlier era commanded such loyalty is that it served many important functions. These functions reinforced feelings of security, identity, and stability. Kinship groups in earlier times were critically important agents in the processes of making a living, providing education, communicating religious traditions, and caring for the infirm and the aged. In recent times most of these responsibilities have been transferred to large formal associations. Union organizations have pension funds, and the government has its responsibilities for health, education, and welfare. Many of the traditional family functions have been taken over by large corporations: Eastman Kodak has its medical plan, IBM its country clubs, du Pont its psychiatrists, Reynolds Tobacco its chaplains—and RCA provides neckties inscribed with the corporate insigne. The modern family is much more dispensable than it used to be, and its loss of function seriously undermines its effectiveness in performing the important responsibilties which remain —to confer identity, adjustment, and affection.

There is another reason why such inordinate demands are made on the modern family: It provides the only long-term associations that many people have. William H. Whyte entitled his chapter about the Organization Man at home in his suburban setting "The Transients." He was calling attention to one of the most important facts about middle-class life. In a nation dominated by symbols of movement and escape—immigration, the frontier, the automobile, and the superhighway—most middle-class homes are "mobile homes" with a vengeance. According to statistics compiled by the U.S. Department of Commerce, half of the American population changes its place of residence every five years. In some states, such as Florida and California, and for many middle-class families, the mobility rates are even higher.

One of the expectations made of the aspiring junior executive working in a large national corporation is that he must be willing to move whenever and wherever the corporation sees fit. The small portable family consisting only of parents and a few children is well suited to the task; it can be moved much more conveniently than the extended kinship family which was common several generations ago. As Warner and Abegglen commented in their study, *Big Business Leaders in America:*

> . . . these are men on the move. They left their home, and all that this implies. They left behind a standard of living, level of income, and style of life to adopt a way of living entirely different from that into which they were born. . . . The physical departure is only a small part of the total process of leaving that a mobile man must undergo. He must leave behind people as well as places. The friends of earlier years must be left, for acquaintances of the lower-status past are incompatible with the successful present. Often the church of his birth is left behind, along with the clubs and cliques of his family and his youth. But most important of all, and this is the great problem of the man on the move, he must, to some degree, leave his father, mother, brothers and sisters, along with the other human relationships of his past.[10]

The real-estate developers who cater to these families on the move are well aware of the perils of transiency and the need to belong. In suburban Park Forest, Illinois, the setting for Whyte's study of the Organization Man, a psychiatrically attuned advertising agency beckoned to the transients with the message that "You *Belong* in PARK FOREST! The moment you come to our town you know you're welcome. You're part of a big group. . . .

You have friends who want you—and you can enjoy being with them." [11] But despite these assurances, rapid mobility is one of the important reasons for feelings of homelessness and uprootedness. It is important to remember that, as I have pointed out before, most of the people attracted to communes come from middle-class homes where frequent moves from one place to another are the rule rather than the exception. If they had chosen the expected career pattern and attempted at least to achieve a status equal to that of their parents, they too would have been expected to move from one place to another as the almost inevitable accompaniment of upward mobility.

These observations also point to another problem that is particularly acute for young people who have left home and, in many cases, also left colleges or universities. Given a population that is highly mobile, in which kin relationships offer little security, in which there are very few associations capable of absorbing unmarried individuals, the marriage relationship becomes pre-eminently important. Until a fairly recent moment in history, religious orders (which in many respects, such as their idealism and renunciation of the world, bear a certain resemblance to the communes) were the approved social path and the available form of community for those who decided not to choose family life. But our society offers almost no alternative to family life. The desperation of unmarried girls in their late twenties and the pity we lavish on the spinster and the widow as well as the "golden ager" cut loose from the bonds of family are evidence of the social vacuum which this society has in store for those who are unmarried or bereaved. A common explanation of the fact that the average age of marriage has continued to decline during the last few decades is that early marriage is less of a financial burden than it used to be. But isn't this also a reflection of the fact that this society offers very few alternatives to marriage and family life? The unattached young people who choose not to follow the normal blueprint of marriage and career are caught in the interstices of the society without any approved communal alternative. It makes very good sense that they should follow Paul Goodman's advice and create a community of their own.

Competitiveness, rapid mobility, and extreme individualism are such familiar features of the American social landscape that we forget what a huge price they exact. The one institution that is supposed to provide a sanctuary of co-operation, affection, and belongingness, the modern family, is peculiarly unsuited to the task. I have sketched a portrait, admittedly brief, of the exaggerated isolation of the middle-class families from which come many of the young people who have chosen to live in communes. It is difficult to imagine a society that more consistently frustrates needs for human interdependence and relatedness than does this one. This helps to explain the enormous appeal of the communal idea to young people coming from families which gave them "everything that money could buy."

In retrospect, the major theme of American social criticism in the fifties seems peculiarly myopic. There was a growing concern about the quality of American life, fear of a widespread loss of individualism, and a surrender to conformity. Dozens of spokesmen for this position argued that the traditional American values—the Protestant ethic of hard work, self-reliance, and rugged individualism— had eroded. According to Archibald MacLeish, there had been "a massive, almost glacial shift away from the passion for individual freedom and toward a desire for security of association, of belonging, of conformity." [12] According to William Whyte, there was a new social ethic of co-operation, a belief in "belongingness" as the ultimate need of the individual. In *The Lonely Crowd*, David Riesman discussed the reasons for a shift from the "inner-directed" personality to the "other-directed" man, concerned above all else with financial security, emotional security, and getting along with others.

But while many of these writers pointed out that character types such as Riesman's "inner-directed" man (recently rechristened "Consciousness I" by Charles Reich) might be historically obsolete, very few of them bothered to notice how deficient American institutions are in catering to needs for belongingness. Despite Riesman's assertion that the modern American is "decisively different" from the Americans whom Tocqueville had observed a century earlier, many of these critics reiterated the Frenchman's sadness about the "universal uniformity [among] this countless multitude of beings, shaped in each other's likenesses." [13] In an acerbic discussion of the lowest-common-denominator quality of American media offerings, Dwight Macdonald stated that "the tendency of modern industrial society, whether in the USA or the USSR, is to transform the individual into the mass man." And he then continued by quoting with approval a comment made by Roger Fry: "It seems to me that nearly the whole Anglo-Saxon race, especially of course in America, have lost the power to be individuals." [14] For many of the other critics of the fifties, the emphasis of the argument was the same: The diagnosis was a surrender to conformity, and the prescription was to rehabilitate the individual, with all of his idiosyncratic quirks.

What these critics didn't notice is that they were encouraging a trait which is already exaggerated in this culture, the assumption that each individual is unique in important ways and that this uniqueness should be carefully defended and cultivated. The same assumption undergirds many visible social conventions, such as private property as an extension of rigidly defined ego boundaries, or our insistence on distancing. Edward T. Hall, the author of a fascinating study of man's use of space, has pointed out that people create insulated private areas around them.[15] The amount of private space that people need in order to feel comfortable varies from one individual to another, and from one country to another. People living in the Mediterranean countries pack much more closely together than do northern Europeans, the English, and Americans. Arabs, as Hall observes, appear to have almost no private space: They have no word to connote privacy, and they flock together in crowds with an abandon that contrasts vividly with the crowd behavior of Americans, such as our self-consciousness in crowded elevators. Americans are a noncontact species.

In its suggested cure for the malaise of the "mass society," the counter culture takes off in a direction entirely different from that of the critics of the fifties. Rather than assuming the uniqueness of the individual and the necessity of defending it, the assumption is, as Freda put it when we were talking in the fields in Taos, that "you and I are one." The emphasis is on what we have in common, not on our individual idiosyncrasies. In the fifties, David Riesman, William Whyte, and others suggested the gradual erosion of individualism in response to new social and economic realities. But the collapse of the individualist assumption in the counter culture is due in large part to the psychedelic experience, which has shattered so many of the ground rules of the mainstream culture.

Our emphasis on intellect is one of the chief reasons why we have carried the assumption of individual differences to such an extreme, while hardly bothering to notice that in most respects people are essentially the same. With his usual insight, Alan Watts commented that our general failure to notice the inseparability of things, and to be aware of our own basic unity with the external world, is the result of specializing in a particular kind of consciousness. For we have largely based culture and civilization on concentrated attention, on using the mind as a spotlight rather than a floodlight, and by this means analyzing the world into separate bits. . . . The price we pay for this vision of the world in vivid detail, bit by bit, is that we lose sight of the relationships and unities between the bits.[16]

One of the perceptual changes that the psychedelic experience typically causes is to dissolve the distinctions that intellect makes between the internal and the external world, to break down ego boundaries, to recapture the experience of unity with others. "There seems to me a strong possibility," said Watts, "that the psychedelics (as a medicine rather than a diet) may help us to 'trigger' a new sense of identity, providing the initial boost to get us out of the habit of restricting 'I' to a vague center within the skin." [17]

If Watts is correct in this conjecture—and I think there is a great deal of evidence that he is—many young people have a radically different sense of identity from that of their elders. The continuity of the social fabric from one generation to the next depends on continuity in the way people look at the world. But one of the effects of this massive ingestion of psychedelics has been a profound shifting of priorities. As a consequence, the conventions of distancing, of creating rigorously defended private spaces, don't make much sense. The effects of psychedelics taken in a group situation are remarkably similar to Nietzsche's Dionysian man experiencing the "primordial unity." To quote Watts again, this time from his magnificent account of a personal experience with psychedelics reported in *The Joyous Cosmology:*

> Members of the group become open to each other
> with a high degree of friendly affection, for in the
> mystical phase of the experience the underlying unity
> or "belongingness" of the members can have all the
> clarity of a physical sensation. Indeed, the social situ-
> ation may become what religious bodies aim at, but
> all too rarely achieve, in their rites of communion—a
> relationship of the most vivid understanding, forgive-
> ness, and love. . . . Between those who enter this
> world together there is also a love which is distinctly
> eucharistic, an acceptance of each other's natures from
> the heights to the depths.[18]

Compared to this ecstatic vision of collective unity, the
day-to-day reality of communal life in most of the groups
is marked by such oppressively normal traits as transient
affections and apathetic do-your-own-thingism. A concern
for breaking down the barriers between people as well as
the attractions of rural life is enough to cause people to
come together in a communal setting, but it is not enough
to keep a group together. Ortega y Gasset once wrote
that "people do not live together merely to be together.
They live together to do something together." [19] This is
more frequently a problem for the rural groups than it is
for their urban counterparts. Most of the urban groups
focus on a particular activity such as radical politics, consumer co-operatives, or craft workshops. But for many of
the rural groups, common activity is limited to part-time
farming. In their permissive climate, there is often a de-
bilitating low-thyroid do-nothingness that looks like nothing so much as the reverse image of the compulsive
busyness of their parents.

One of the important reasons for the vitality of the
Israeli collectives, the kibbutzim, especially in earlier
years, was the commitment to Zionism, the shared task of
carving a life out of the desert and creating a defense outpost against the common enemy.[20] In the absence of such

shared long-term tasks and commitments, there is in many communes really no community at all. "The real essence of community," Martin Buber said, "is to be found in the fact . . . that it has a center. The real beginning of a community is when its members have a common relation to the centre overriding all other relations." [21] But in this current reaction against the depersonalization of the mainstream society, "liberation" is defined in the Elysian terms of total freedom rather than the more realistic sense of new responsibilities. Repeating the quintessentially American trait, when conditions of communal life become intolerable, the residents simply move elsewhere. As a consequence, there is a very rapid rate of turnover in commune membership and a short average life-span for many groups. Among the rural communes, the average life-span is not much longer than that of the Fourierist colonies a hundred years ago, one to two years.

The dilemma is summarized in this poignant note which was pinned up on a communal bulletin board:

> I hope that this week is the Farm's lowest point for the summer, because if it gets any lower I don't think I have a decent place to live. . . . I think of this as my (at least) temporary home. And I like my home to be clear of broken glass and papers, my tools and supplies put away, I like to keep track of my guests, take care of my animals. . . . But this farm is far from that. . . .
>
> Our average farmer (Asshole) says to himself: "I'm here visiting (for a day, a week, a month, or a year) and I'm not really a part of this farm, just a guest, so I can't do anything really effective about the Farm's condition."
>
> I believe the key to the problem is: STABILITY LEADS TO A FEELING OF COMMUNITY.
>
> We have very little sense of community here. . . . This is social decay: where the natural forces of the family (helping, loving, working together) are driven

out by the selfishness. . . . I believe that the decay, the pigs-at-the-trough feeling, is caused by the instability.

When a stable group of ten lives together for weeks, natural forces work *for* community feeling. When the Farm is more than 20 per cent tourists, when the family feeling is broken every day or two by departures and arrivals, I see no hope.[22]

As Robert Owen remarked when New Harmony collapsed in the 1820's, "The habits of the individual system die hard." The lessons of "the individual system" place little emphasis on sharing, co-operation, and interdependence. Most of the successful communitarian groups of the last century and this one have adopted special techniques to air grievances and reinforce feelings of group unity, to educate people for group living. I mentioned in Chapter Two that the Oneida colony practiced a form of group therapy that they called "mutual criticism." In another very successful group, the Bruderhof community, a different technique is used for the same purpose, to prevent gossip or "backbiting": The "first law" of the Bruderhof community is that a judgment made of anyone in the group must be made directly to that person. Another interpersonal technique which the group has devised is a procedure for catharsis. Everyone in the brotherhood has the right to ring the gong, to call the members together at anytime, and "clear the air," to state his grievances or make a confession of guilt. One of the group's most important rules is a prohibition against returning to any action which has been "cleared." [23] Om'ing before every collective meeting and a variety of the Esalen-developed techniques for sensory communion are widely used. And many communes have invented ceremonies to reinforce feelings of group solidarity. For example, at Libre, one of the Colorado communes, childbirth is ritualized. Whenever possible, delivery takes place outside with the entire group chanting to welcome the infant into his new environment.

Liberté, Égalité, Fraternité . . . and *Sexualité.* As one of the great revolutionary symbols, sexual liberation takes its place along with the other three demands. To listen to Abbie Hoffman's vision of the new society, it apparently becomes the most important of all:

> We will fly the flag of nothingness over the Pentagon and a mighty cheer of liberation will echo through the land. "We are free, Great God Almighty, Free at last." Schoolchildren will rip out their desks and throw ink at stunned instructors, office secretaries will disrobe and run into the streets, newsboys will rip up their newspapers and sit on the curbstones masturbating. . . . "The War is over. Let's get some ass." [24]

Or to recall the words of the Marquis de Sade in Weiss's play: "What's the purpose of revolution without general copulation?"

The contempt with which many revolutionary movements have attempted to dismiss both conventional morality and the marriage relationship is by now familiar. It was one of the prominent reasons for the infamy of many of the American communitarian insurrections in the nineteenth century. The Mormons were chased from one settlement to another more than halfway across the continent chiefly because of their habit of polygyny. The Shakers deviated from the conventional sexual morality, but in a different direction, by imposing celibacy. They were so sure that the end of the world was imminent that they saw no need to perpetuate the species. Mother Ann Lee, the founder of the cult, who considered herself a female incarnation of Christ, fulminated against consummated marriage as "a covenant with death and an agreement with hell," and branded any act of congress as "filthy gratification." [25]

But of all these communitarian experiments, the Perfectionists at the Oneida Community anticipated most nearly the counter-cultural ideal of a completely non-repressive civilization in which sex is released from its bondage in monogamous marriage. In the "Battle-Ax Letter," Father Noyes pointed out that, according to Biblical authority, in the Kingdom of God there would be no marriage. Since it is necessary in this life to prepare for the next, the community practiced the ideal of unselfish, unpossessive mutual love. For Noyes, the socialist principle applied equally to property and people. "We affirm that there is no intrinsic difference between property in persons and property in things, and that the same spirit which abolished exclusiveness in regard to money would abolish, if circumstances allowed full scope to it, exclusiveness in regard to women and children. . . . The possessive feeling which expresses itself by the possessive pronoun *mine* is the same in essence when it relates to women as when it relates to money or any other property." [26] Noyes's idea was that by discouraging any tendencies toward the exclusive possession by one person of another and by expanding the scope of sexual activities, the intimacy which is normally confined to the nuclear family could be extended to a much larger group. This ideal has been expressed many times, but the extraordinary thing about the Oneida Community is that it successfully practiced group marriage for several decades.

In practice, group marriage as a means of enhancing collective unity hasn't fared well in the counter culture. From the point of view of some people, the lofty ideal of group marriage is no more than a smoke screen for baser motives. Witness the words of Valerie Solanas, no admirer of men in any case, in the SCUM Manifesto:

The "hippy" . . . who is excited by the thought of
having lots of women accessible to him, rebels against
the harshness of a Breadwinner's life and the monotony of one woman. In the name of sharing and cooperation, he forms the commune or tribe. The commune,
being an extended family, is an extended violation of females' rights, privacy and sanity, and is no
more a community than normal "society." The most
important activity of the commune, the one on which
it is based, is gangbanging.

The habits of the individual system die hard, but none
so hard as this one: that two people—paired off—*belong*
to one another. Despite the counter culture's commitment
to liberation and nonrepressive sexuality, most of the
groups practice a familar form of serial monogamy. This
is perhaps the most surprising thing about sex in the
communes, that in reaction to a generation that was
nearly fanatical in its denial of sex, and in response to the
ministrations of the media in which sex is the most important incentive in the art of merchandising, the sexual
practices of many of the communes should be so thoroughly conventional.

The habit of pairing off is opposed to the commitment
to the group in several ways, and it accounts for the re-
luctance that most groups have to admit that serial
monogamy is practised. Melford Spiro commented on
this problem in his discussion of the kibbutz:

The reason for this public "denial" of a strong bond
between partners seems to have been twofold. In the
first place, to have acted otherwise would have been
"bourgeois" and the kibbutz viewed bourgeois behavior as a stigma. Secondly, Kiryat Yedidim [the
settlement that Spiro studied] emphasized group living as an end in itself, so that the individual's strongest tie was supposed to be with the entire community.
It was, therefore, important for a person who had

acquired a "companion" to emphasize the fact that he had not divorced himself from the group life, and that he was not creating a private life or developing private interests that would sever his ties with the group.[27]

In the communes, there is the same desire to avoid the stigma of holding "bourgeois" attitudes and to deny that any single relationship is more important than commitment to the whole group.

The idea that communal life is a sexual smörgåsbord is a myth created and sustained by the media. Much of the media fascination with Charles Manson and his covey of willing women can be explained by the fact that he personally staged many men's fondest sexual fantasies. One of the popular stories about Manson's Promethean sexual prowess described his daily activities. Manson would get up in the morning, make love, eat breakfast, make love, and go back to sleep. Then he would wake up again, make love, have lunch, make love, and take a nap. Waking up a while later, he would make love, eat dinner, make love, and go back to sleep, only to wake up in the middle of the night looking for a willing partner. By normal standards, such a strenuous routine is too much of a good thing. But for all the attention that the Manson cult received, it was certainly not "typical" in any way of commune life in general.

There are several indications of widespread interest in group marriage which extends far beyond the counter culture. More than one-quarter of the twenty thousand readers of *Psychology Today* who responded to a recent poll were interested in, or in favor of, some form of group marriage.[28] And the writings of Robert Rimmer, the Norman Vincent Peale of the group-marriage idea, continue to attract a large audience. In one of his early books, *The Rebellion of Yale Marrott,* Rimmer posed the dilemma of a man who finds himself married to two women, both of whom he loves. A relationship is worked out so that all three live together in contented polygamy—until the authorities step in and charge Yale with bigamy. Though many middle-aged people have never heard of it, Rimmer's next book, *The Harrad Experiment*, has become part of the folklore of the younger generation. The novel recounts the adventures of six students at Harrad College, a mythical institution which stresses the importance of learning about love and sexuality and encourages experimentation with new life styles. Philip Tenhausen, the college's president, tells his incoming students, "If a few men could find the answers to the sexual confusions of modern times and make people aware that hate and jealousy are not instinctive behavior but learned reactions, then they will have at least created an outpost in the jungle of human inter-relationships." A more recent novel, *Proposition Thirty-one*, deals with a proposal to amend the laws of California to permit corporate marriage. Rimmer has no illusions, though, about instantly converting the American public to the idea of group marriage. In his opinion, most Americans are not yet psychologically ready for the idea.[29]

Judging from the experience of the groups that have experimented with it, even people who are enthusiastic about group marriage have serious problems making it work. One of the groups, called Harrad West, lives in Berkeley near the campus. Their statement of what they are trying to achieve as an alternative to the nuclear family, as it appeared in the magazine *Sexual Freedom*, echoes many of the sentiments of the Oneida colony:

> Our basic idea at Harrad West is that perhaps six, eight, or even a dozen or more adults can form "marriage" relationships with each other as a means of attaining far more than monogamous marriage can offer in the way of healthy, creative, and stimulating fulfillment. Aside from the high divorce rate, the large number of unstimulating or downright unhappy mar-

riages attest to the fact that monogamy often leaves much to be desired. . . . A larger number of concerned persons learning and growing together often can deal with stresses that overwhelm two individuals. . . . We believe that sexual relationships are vital and that a marriage rarely succeeds without them. We have discovered that sharing one's mate in return for sharing someone else for a time actually enhances the pair bond relationship. We feel that our friendships have deepened, our capacity for warmth and understanding increased and our lives enriched as a result of this.

The idea is that all of the adult members of the group are considered to be married to all the adults of the opposite sex. "Pair bond" relationships are recognized since most of the members joined the community as couples. (One of the couples has been married for seventeen years and has three children.) But, theoretically at least, the members' primary commitment is to the whole group.

As a female member of Harrad West explains it, "One of our goals in setting this thing up was to provide a better environment for our children. This arrangement gives quite a bit more freedom to the parents—you're not stuck with the kids all the time and they're not stuck with you." As far as possessions are concerned, most of the large investments such as appliances are owned collectively, but each of the members reserves some private belongings.

Predictably, the group's hardest problem has been to avoid conflicts and to maintain intimacy and openness among all the members. For a period of nine months, a trained therapist met weekly with the group to help in self-exploration and to teach people how to communicate their differences. After experimenting both with spontaneous and planned sex, the group worked out a schedule for rotating partners. "We've tried it both ways," one of the women said, "and found that it works better to know ahead of time who you'll be sleeping with. We spend two or three nights a week with our pair bond partner, and one night a week with each other member of the opposite sex. Sex every night is not a must, and spontaneity is not ruled out—especially during the day."

But like so many of the other experiments, at last report the future of Harrad West was in jeopardy. One of the members was forced to leave because of "adolescent tantrums," and since then several others have left. As one of the original members put it, "Well, we're about as permanent as regular marriages generally are here in California. We've spent an incredible amount of time and energy on maintaining the group, and we've had some problems. But I'm sure I'll never return to a monogamous relationship." [30]

So what can we conclude about this collective quest, other than to notice so often at the bottom of the intoxicating cup of community the dregs of discord, selfishness, and jealousy? In many ways the young, for all their communitarian instincts, are very poorly equipped for the task of living intimately with several dozen people. In any case, the task of learning new ways of relating to people and forming a society from scratch is a huge responsibility. In comparison, the problem of effecting political change seems fairly easy.

How many critics have dismissed the communitarian experiments as an irresponsible retreat from the "real problems" of the society? And how many people have predicted that after the failure of such hopelessly utopian ventures, the young will return to the more practical social arrangements offered by the mainstream society? Despite the institutional weakness of the modern family and the ways in which this society frustrates the needs for interdependence and community, to suggest that we should encourage such experiments in alternative social arrangements is viewed as a major heresy. We are constantly reminded in Sunday-supplement sociology that this is an era of rapid social change. Yet despite the fact that old social solutions begin to smell like three-day-old fish, the modern family, which developed in response to strikingly different conditions from those of the mid-twentieth century, has an army of avid defenders. Aside from the enormous weight of institutional inertia, there are marriage counselors, women's magazines, and pulpit messages, all intended to remind us that with a little bit of individual effort every family can attain the contented turgidity of the "Ozzie and Harriet" or the "Father Knows Best" model. The laws not only recognize the existence of the nuclear family, they effectively eliminate the opposition. The housing developments (each unit with three bedrooms: for Mom and Dad, and the kids) and the new apartment buildings (mainly studios for young singles not yet ready to move into the housing developments) reinforce the social conventions of privacy and distancing.

But where are we to look for ideas about what the alternatives might be—to the nineteenth-century experiments, to the tribal style of the American Indians, to the kibbutzim? David Riesman once commented that "we assume that all possible forms of human relatedness have already been experienced, so that if the present forms are unsatisfying, then better ones must be looked for in our own past." [31] But to talk of "retribalizing" is at best to speak analogously. It is very natural to look to the past for suggestions about what alternative social arrangements might work, but because the problems of the present age are, at least in part, new ones, the solutions must be new ones too.

Any new social arrangements will have to respond to at least four tendencies that I think we can safely assume will become more widespread in the future: (1) There appears to be a trend away from a lifelong commitment to family and domestic concerns; (2) there will probably be more willingness to allow considerable individual choice about both the extent and the duration of intimate relationships; (3) the idea of shared children—children who are not socialized exclusively by their parents—will become more popular; and (4) we can probably expect that many of the negative emotions associated with marriage—such as exclusiveness, possessiveness, and jealousy—will decrease.

But even if these changes come about, the assumption that monogamous marriage is the *only* secure arrangement that can satisfy needs for affection, companionship, and sex will begin to disappear only *after* there is some available alternative. The collective experiments in the counter culture don't yet provide a real alternative. But they do point to what I think is the most attractive alternative to the nuclear family—extended nonfamily forms of relationship that provide both security and variety.

8 : "Simplify, Simplify"

> Why should we be in such desperate haste to succeed,
> and in such desperate enterprises?
> —Thoreau

> The great question, about which hangs a true sub-
> limity, and the terror of overhanging fate, is: what are
> you going to do with all these things? What is to be
> the end of which these are to be the means?
> —Thomas Henry Huxley

> Our life is frittered away by detail . . . simplify,
> simplify.
> —Thoreau

In 1967, Paul Goodman wrote a prophetic piece entitled
"Rural Life: 1984." He looked back from the perspective
of the mid-1980's to the rural reconstruction movement
which had begun a decade earlier and threatened to in-
undate Vermont with successive waves of young people
fleeing from the cities. It seems that what everyone had
predicted had finally happened: Cities began to collapse
under the burden placed on them by the twentieth century. The only unexpected thing about the Summer of
Seven Plagues was that everything went wrong all at
once. It started with a transit strike in one of the large

urban areas which caused the streets to be glutted with traffic. And then, in the midst of the crisis, there was a thermal invasion and forty thousand people died from the smog. On the next day there was a power failure. A week later, the city water system sprang a leak and ten million people were affected by the drought. Whether it was just bad luck or some kind of chain reaction, a few days later the new SST, on its maiden voyage, overshot the runway and plunged into the skyscrapers. And finally there was the great riot, because it *had* been one very long, hot summer. After this magnificent demonstration of what people had suspected for at least a decade, that cities were both unlivable and unmanageable, millions of young people were heard muttering the same thing: "Zap! This urban area has put the whammies on me!" Thus began the rural reconstruction movement. Social engineers pointed out that the same solution that had worked for the "Indian problem" might work for the "young radical problem." Accordingly, with a certain expedient wisdom, the administration decided to stop harassing the nonconformist young and instead encouraged rural reservations for them. The CIA even picked up the bill for their transportation. And that, from the perspective of 1984, seems to explain the incredible patchquilt of new settlements throughout Vermont preoccupied with subsistence farming, inauthentic mountain music, and environmental activism.[1]

This essay is just one example of Goodman's gift as a visionary sociologist. Surely someone in Washington must already be thinking about government subsidies for rural reservations for the radical minority. Goodman's only mistake was in his timing. Parts of Vermont (not to mention New Mexico, Oregon, California, and several other states) already resemble his colonies of Diggers. But in his anticipation of a wholesale rejection of urban life and a turn toward voluntary primitivism, Goodman couldn't have predicted more accurately what has happened since he wrote the essay in 1967.

The setting of almost all the early utopias was the city, where the good life meant the life abundant. None of the utopian writers was thinking of anything so vast as modern urban areas. But to be civilized literally means to be a city-dweller, and for any of the early utopian writers to assume that the good life could take place anywhere else would have been unimaginable. There is something profoundly important in the fact that this contemporary vision of the good life identifies the good with that which is natural, completely unencumbered by civilization.

The primitivist ideal reverses all the assumptions of the idea of progress. Primitivism looks backward to a time when life was simpler; progress looks forward to a time when life will be better. During the nineteenth century and the first few decades of this one, progress, the belief that mankind is steadily advancing toward a higher standard of living, was a captivating idea. Human ingenuity was triumphant. Science was adding each day to the stock of man's knowledge of the world in which he lived. During a period of just a few decades, new discoveries and achievements made dramatic changes in everyday life: Fewer children died as infants; people lived longer, were better housed and fed. Dozens of inventions such as the refrigerator, the telegraph, and the railroad were visible achievements which made life easier for millions of people. Capitalism found its ethical justification in the fact that it encouraged new inventions and greater productivity. New and better things meant that men could live more comfortably.

In America in the mid-twentieth century, the idea of progress and all the other justifications for hard work and acquisitiveness have far outlived any evidence that new products and inventions are anything more than un-

necessary complications of our lives. Yet, since so many
people are occupied with the task of creating a market
for new things and more things, we are encouraged not
to think about such fundamentally illogical facts as
built-in obsolescence or an annual expenditure of nearly
twenty billion dollars on advertising. In an economy
geared to frantic consumption, nothing is to be feared
so much as the possibility that people will stop buying.
A leading investment banker considered the possibility
a few years ago and characteristically concluded by
worrying about the market:

> Clothing would be purchased for its utility; food
> would be bought on the basis of economy and nutri-
> tional value; automobiles would be stripped to essen-
> tials and held by the same owners for the full 10 to
> 15 years of their useful lives; homes would be built
> and maintained for their characteristics of shelter,
> without regard to style or neighborhood. And what
> would happen to a market dependent upon new mod-
> els, new styles, new ideas? [2]

In *Island*, Aldous Huxley's fictional paradise based on
spiritual and communal values, one of the characters who
wants to sabotage this best of all possible worlds thinks
about bringing in millions of Sears, Roebuck catalogs to
whet the natives' appetite for possessions. Huxley's fiction
was never far from fact. Franklin D. Roosevelt once said
that if he could place one American book in the hands
of every Russian, the volume of his choice would be a
Sears, Roebuck catalog. Such is the stuff of American
dreams.

In a society addicted to consumption, work becomes
addictive too. A puzzled Eric Hoffer wrote that

> in practically all civilizations we know of, and in the
> Occident too, for many centuries work was viewed

as a curse, a mark of bondage, or, at best, a necessary evil. That free men shoud be willing to work day after day, even after their vital needs are satisfied, and that work should be seen as a mark of uprightness and manly worth, is not only unparalleled in history but remains more or less incomprehensible to many people outside the Occident.[3]

The primitivist style implies a rejection of the city, consumerism, technology, and the compulsion to work. It is based on a thoroughly subversive assumption. The calculus of capitalism suggests that the ultimate problem is to maintain full employment at noninflationary levels in order to turn out as many things as the economy can absorb. In the counter culture this logic is reversed: The problem is to calculate the minimum of labor necessary in order to satisfy the essential needs of everyone in the society. Like the worker's motto in Morris' *News From Nowhere,* the cry is, "Now at last we will produce no more for profit but for *use,* for *happiness,* for LIFE."

The essence of the counter culture's critique is that in a society so engorged with things people become an extension of, or at best servants to, their possessions. People define themselves in terms of their things, the cars they drive, the cigarettes they smoke. The rhythm of modern life imitates the rhythm of the productive process. As Thoreau put it, these lives of quiet desperation are "minced into hours and fretted by the ticking of the clock." The things that not long ago were clearly our servants have somehow gained the upper hand. This is the premonition of the late-night monster movies: The clever scientist is finally terrorized by his creation.

The solution? The simple life. Homesteading. A conscious program of trying to live with as few things as possible. Giving up electricity, the telephone, running water, washing machines. Getting close to the earth. Building houses out of mud or trees. Making homemade bread. Raising organic gardens. And all the while quoting Thoreau, chapter and verse: "It would be some advantage to live a primitive and frontier life, though in the midst of an outward civilization, if only to learn what are the gross necessaries of life. . . ."

But there's one very widespread idea that Thoreau never thought about, the current conviction that civilization is going to self-destruct and that the primitive style is a means of self-preservation. As one seventeen-year-old girl who had just escaped from suburban Los Angeles explained it: "When the country is wiped out, there's not going to be any more electricity, right? And there's not going to be anyone to fix your machines. In order to survive, we're just going to have to depend upon ourselves. So we're trying to do all those things right now. We're trying to get rid of all the machines that we can't fix ourselves. You've really got to be prepared." Stewart Brand, the editor of the *Whole Earth Catalog*, wrote, "One barometer of people's social-confidence level is the sales of books on survival. I can report that sales on *The Survival Book* are booming: it's one of our fastest-moving items."

A glance at the *Whole Earth Catalog*, now defunct (though not for lack of readers), or at any of its successors suggests the flavor of the whole movement. It was a kind of underground Sears, Roebuck catalog, except that rather than hawking the newest, the biggest, and the most expensive, it did just the opposite. And in the process, it was helpful in a hip avuncular way which suggested that survival might be possible after all. It even contained a statement of purpose, something that the Sears people don't do:

A realm of intimate personal power is developing—
power of the individual to conduct his education, find
his own inspiration, stage his own environment, and
share his adventure with whoever is interested. Tools
that aid this process are sought and promoted by the
Whole Earth Catalog.

So it was a tool chest. Let's suppose that you want to
make yourself a genuine buckskin shirt. Since buckskin
isn't much in demand at the local department store, the
catalog suggests that you write to the Leather Tanning
Company in San Francisco and includes all the details.
Or maybe you're worrying about phosphate pollution
from laundry detergents and want to know which products to buy. There are also advertisements for such books
as *Survival Arts of the Primitive Paiutes,* an *Untitled
Epic Poem on the History of Industrialization,* and something called *Village Planning in the Primitive World.* In
case you're interested, there are instructions for a fifty-
dollar do-it-yourself burial ("Human bodies are an organic part of the whole earth and at death must return
to the ongoing stream of life . . ."). And there are articles
on Buckminster Fuller's World Game, instructions on bee
keeping, how to build your own cistern, advice on the
manufacture of homemade wine, and a choice of five
diagrams for your own teepee. In short, everything that
middle-class youngsters never learned at home.

The successors to the *Whole Earth Catalog* run the
same kinds of items. For example, from the *Mother Earth
News,* an article on "My $25.00 Log Cabin." (Thoreau
would have been delighted: his cost twenty-eight dollars,
and that was more than a hundred years ago.) Or another, an article on shopping at the dump entitled "The
Fine Art of Trashmongering," written by the members
of the Heathcote Community in Maryland. Their idea is
that in such an immodestly endowed society there's treas-

ure in trash. The article includes a partial inventory of one evening's plunder:

1. An elegant and durable stuffed lion, intact but for one eye and needing only the washing machine to be like new.
2. A Frito Bandito pencil.
3. A toy watering can, new condition.
4. A small boy's blue blazer, nearly new condition, and emblazoned with the words "College Bound," which we removed.[4]

The Heathcote gang admitted that these were fairly modest pickings, but after all, it's a start in their program of "debourgeoisification," the task of becoming a nonconsumer. As they are all fond of recalling on their visits to the dump, the Lord helps those who help themselves.

In the midst of this campaign to regain the simple life, naturalness is one of the strongest themes. On most of the farms, voluntary primitivism means exactly that: There are no tractors; everything is done by hand, organically. Anything that's artificial is regarded with high suspicion. But having grown up in a world where so little was natural, it takes a while for some of the new recruits to sort out what is and what isn't. In one of the Taos communes, a girl was going on at length about how the group could make it without any power tools, without artificial fertilizers, without *anything* from the plastic world outside. A few minutes later, someone was leaving for a "milk run" to the nearest store (they didn't have any cows or goats) and asked her if she needed anything. She answered that she'd been out of Breck hair rinse for a week and asked him to pick up a bottle.

For all these lapses, the emphasis on naturalness begins with a perception that is critically important, a newfound ecological consciousness, an awareness of the war that Western man has been waging against nature. At its fringes, this cult of naturalness has a way of shading off into absurdity. In Charles Reich's *The Greening of America,* the normal supermarket types of artificial peanut butter are portrayed as one of the major atrocities committed by the Corporate Conspiracy.

This emphasis on what is natural and the unwillingness to make any compromises with technology or the necessities of commerce create a serious problem. Very few of the communes have either craft industries or any other profit-making business. The garden is the center of most of the groups' economic life, providing much of the daily food supply. The economy is often supplemented by the use of food stamps and income from day labor in nearby jobs such as crop picking or fire fighting. Most of the group, however, are not economically self-sufficient. They have to depend on two sources of money that come in from outside: money taken from savings or sent by parents, and gifts and donations from visitors and new members. Twin Oaks, the Walden Two-oriented group in Virginia, is a notable exception. They have a thriving hammock-making industry and are planning an assortment of other small industries such as an electronic-parts business. But for most of the other groups, the commitment to a simple life in the country means farming, which is difficult and often boring. Nietzsche was not the only nineteenth-century writer to criticize the contemporary utopian colonies for their dullness, insipidness, and uneventfulness. Marx dismissed the whole thing as "rural idiocy." In his survey of the nineteenth-century American experiments, John Humphrey Noyes warned against farming for very practical reasons:

> We incline to think that this fondness for land, which has been the habit of socialists had much to do with their failures. Farming is about the hardest and longest of all roads to fortune. . . . We should have advised the phalanxes to limit their landholdings to a minimum

and put their strength as soon as possible into some form of manufacture.[5]

This is advice that the counter-culture communes are unlikely to follow. For all the ways in which these groups would like to be economically self-sufficient, to follow the Twin Oaks example and create small industries means to be implicated in the whole economic system. In this struggle between doctrinal purity and economic self-sufficiency, the first concern is more important, at least as long as most of the groups continue to receive subsidies from outside.

Aside from the undoubtedly faddish popularity of much of the current ecological awareness, the assumption that many young people are making about man's place in the natural world is one of the most radical ideas that the counter culture bears. It reverses the typically Western assumption that nature is something inanimate and external to man, something to be mastered and used.

It is interesting to compare the origin myths of Christianity with those of any of the primitive peoples for whom man is a partner in the universe. For the Hopi, for example, the origin myth stresses the importance of the original wisdom granted to man, that the earth is a living entity. The purpose of the religious ceremonies prescribed in the myth is to help maintain the harmony of the universe. Each Hopi child learns that he is a citizen of the natural world as well as an earthly family and a tribal clan. In contrast, the Christian origin myth says that man was made in the image of God, and was given dominion over nature.

Even in the West, influenced by this anthropocentric conception of the universe, the awe which restrained primitive man from injuring the earth or changing its shape was in evidence until fairly recently. Its traces are found in agricultural practices and certain acts of conciliation and consecration which used to follow the completion of man-made structures, suggesting that there had been an act of desecration. For the most part, though, the Western attitude toward nature has been exactly the opposite of the Hopi attitude. There is no thought of a single spiritual essence which pervades every part of the natural world. Nearly every part of the earth now bears the mark of the belief that nature was given to man to use and despoil. Our relation to nature is more like forcible rape than intercourse between two consenting parties.

The art and craft of the primitive shaman was to communicate with the forces of nature as with another equal and respected member of the universe. When it was necessary for man to use nature—to hunt or to take food out of the earth—it was approached with reverence. Its permission was obtained through the use of ritual, and the partnership between man and nature was kept intact. Many of the rituals of the rural communes revive this ancient sense of partnership in the universe. This is how Peter Rabbit, a member of one of the Colorado communes, describes his hunting:

> I don't know anything about sporty hunting. I'm a good poacher. I've thought a lot about it and decided that if there's going to be meat on our table I'm going to put it there. I hunt with a .22 Winchester magnum with a 4x scope. I have a blind overlooking a big block of salt in a creek bottom. The deers come there every morning and evening. I watch them. I call them with a Herter's Deer Call. I ask them if any among them is ready to die. I tell them that we will use the energy we get from eating their flesh in a way that would please them. I don't forget those words. Almost always it is a doe without a fawn or a lone buck that tells me he will join us. I shoot them in the chest from no further than 50 yards. They die almost instantly. I feel

their spirit enters me everytime. It feels good. That's all I know about killing deer.

Most people, of course, dismiss such gestures as magic and superstition, as "bad science." To primitive people who know nothing about our science but a great deal about the natural world, Peter Rabbit's hunting ritual would be a perfectly understandable way of recognizing "the spirit of the earth." [6]

It is a strange sort of radicalism that looks back to the primitive shaman for its inspiration. But it is by importing such unfamiliar ideas that the counter culture has begun to strike down such basic features of our society as the assumptive apparatus of science and industrial civilization and its infatuation with growth and progress.

Whenever I hear young radicals voicing their distaste for industrial civilization I imagine C. P. Snow rushing in to criticize them—the same way that he criticized the intellectuals—as ungrateful heirs of the industrial revolution. In his essay on the "two cultures" he bitterly attacked the intellectuals who refuse to acknowledge the extent to which science had enriched human life and relieved the suffering of the masses, a failure which he attributed to the intellectuals' ignorance of science.[7] Much of what he had to say about the intellectuals applies as well to the dissident young. It is true that many of them are reflexive Luddites out to smash the machines. It was not the new machines that were responsible for the low wages and unemployment in England in the first decades of the nineteenth century which triggered the Luddite campaign. The Luddites were wrong in their rejection of technology and so also in many ways are the disaffected young. It is as false to regard technology as demonic and destructive as it is to regard it with sanguine optimism.

Material abundance and the present state of technology are the indispensable preconditions of this revolt. This is the reason why the critics of the counter culture who repeat C. P. Snow's argument miss the point. Snow defended industrialization against the attacks of such men as William Morris, Thoreau, and D. H. Lawrence, arguing that their rejection of technology was indefensibly elitist. His contention makes very good sense in an economy of scarcity still primarily concerned with attaining the goal of universal prosperity. But the moral claim which Snow attached to the attainment of a higher material standard of living has lost its urgency, in large part because that goal has already been achieved. The dedication to technology and acquisitiveness which was appropriate in an era of scarcity is outmoded now.

Even if the dissident young have not as yet formulated an alternative to complete submission to technology or rejection of it, there is an essential wisdom in their critique. Having moved beyond the era of scarcity, the most important thing is not to allow the imperatives of technology to invade every aspect of our lives. What Kenneth Keniston called the "growing bankruptcy of technological values and visions" poses a huge problem for the young.[8] Maybe it is only by choosing a life of voluntary primitivism—or, as Thoreau put it, learning what are "the gross necessaries of life"—that they can begin to define a new vision of a society that transcends technology.

9 : *The Search for Alternative Realities*

Our civilization represses not only the instincts, not only sexuality, but any form of transcendence. Among one-dimensional men, it is not surprising that someone with an insistent experience of other dimensions, that he cannot entirely deny or forget, will run the risk either of being destroyed by the others, or of betraying what he knows. . . . I would wish to emphasize that our "normal," "adjusted" state is too often the abdication of ecstasy, the betrayal of our true potentialities, that many of us are only too successful in acquiring a false self to adapt to false realities.

—R. D. Laing

Just after nightfall, when the profile of the Sangre de Cristo Mountains can no longer be seen looming in the distance and the first cool breeze sweeps across the valley, the worshipers file one by one into the ceremonial teepee, walking clockwise around the fire and the crescent altar shaped out of earth and clay, and sit down in a circle around its edges. Then Little Joe, the "roadman," the ritual leader, an ancient Pueblo Indian, his leathery face mapped with creases, enters and mutters the first prayer. "I am going into my place of worship. Be with us tonight, Father Peyote." Carrying a long staff and a gourd rattle in one hand and a small leather bag in the other, he sits down, legs crossed, on the far side of the teepee in front of the raised altar, pours some Bull Durham into cornhusk "papers," and passes both around the circle. As the smoke from his cigarette rises through the flap in the top of the teepee, he prays to the earth creator, Father Peyote. Several men sitting around the dimly lit circle add their prayers for guidance, asking for help in following the peyote road. Then, exactly the same way that the ceremony of the peyote religion has proceeded for hundreds of years, Little Joe sprinkles dry cedar on the fire, makes four ritual passes of the peyote bag, takes out several buttons for himself, and passes the rest. Following his lead, everyone chews the bitter, shriveled cactus buttons. Then the roadman holds the staff at arm's length between his body and the fire, shakes the rattle in his right hand, and calls for the opening song. The water drum, which is passed from one person to the next around the circle, accompanies the chants and songs. At first the chants consist of recognizable words repeated over and over: "Jesus is the only way," or "I know Jesus now." And then, as the peyote has its effect and brings the power to commune with the spirits, the fire flickers into a thousand unimagined whirling colors, and the chants become fervent, wailing appeals. The singers sway back and forth, eyes upward, their voices an intermediary for powers beyond. Tear-choked, they ask the Peyote Father for health, for rain, for forgiveness, for the gift of love. The drum and the staff pass round and round the circle, songs and chants alternating with prayers and visions until the first hint of dawn shows through the teepee many hours later. . . . What is remarkable about the ceremony is that, with the exception of Little Joe, none of the worshipers are Indians. They are the members of one of the Taos communes. For most of them, these monthly peyote meetings are the most important events in the group's life. As one of the males in the group put it, "These meetings are what holds the community together. Every time it's a beautiful day the next morning."

On a farm in Texas, a group that calls itself the Children of God practices a form of Christianity that includes Holy Roller hymn singing and a fundamentalist, old-time-religion emphasis on hellfire and retribution. It was founded by twenty-one-year-old Jonathan Levi and his younger sister, Faith, after three years of itinerant preaching, collecting followers from the flotsam of the youth culture who were determined to live God's way. "I'd been searching for an answer, something to give meaning to my life," said one of the Children, the nineteen-year-old daughter of a wealthy businessman. "I tried drugs, Zen, a dozen other things, but none of it worked. Then I met the Children of God, and I just gave up everything and joined them. I knew this wasn't just a way of passing time on Sunday, this was God's truth being lived."

We had been sitting around a table after dinner in the lodge at one of the Oregon communes, discussing what it was that had changed so quickly. After an hour or so, one of the younger girls offered an explanation that everyone seemed to agree with: "Just look at how badly things have been fucked up with this rationality trip. Everyone was tricked into thinking that that was the whole game. But that's just not where it's *at*. What makes all of us in this new generation so different is our God thirst. We've been exposed to entirely new vibes, and we're living in an entirely different kind of reality."

They are indeed. Anyone who lives on the border between "straight" society and the counter culture or, worse yet, anyone who attempts to move between them is likely to get a bad case of the cognitive bends. It is rather like stepping from one civilization into another and finding that reality has been drastically redefined. Everything that is taken most seriously in one world is at best laughable in the other.

The ratified version of reality in the mainstream culture is ruthlessly one-dimensional. Western man has specialized in one form of consciousness, a rational, scientific way of looking at the world. For some time now we have been engaged in a form of scientific imperialism that not only ignores the nonintellective capacities of man but denies them entirely. Science has an "explanation" for any sort of ecstatic experience, and not a very flattering one at that.

In the communes, and in the other provinces where the counter culture's version of reality is taken seriously, science and rationality give way to the nonrational, the supernatural, the unplumbed depths of the visionary experience, and an ambitious search for ecstatic experience. The most cherished insights of this cognitive minority—such as the mystic insistence on the unity of the whole universe—as well as its less exalted insights are inaccessible to the normal everyday conciousness.

What started several years ago with the growing popularity of Zen is now an outrageous assortment consisting of the most venerable religious traditions side by side with dozens of cults and crazes. The list now includes Scientology, Abilitism, light radiation, Sufism, psychocybernetics, astral projection, the 3H (Happy, Healthy, Holy) Organization founded by Yogi Bhajan, transcendental meditation, Kundalini yoga, and the use of alphawave headsets. And that's only the *beginning* of the list. Witchcraft, sorcery, and the occult abound. Many of the communes make major decisions by consulting the *I Ching*. The life of more than one of the groups is punctuated by rumors of UFO's. One young man, who should be an authority on such things, informed me that he was a messenger from another planet. Whatever else such a list suggests, it is evidence of what Theodore Roszak called "the search for alternative realities." Only a small minority of the communes consist of members of a single religious persuasion such as the Children of God, where the group's purpose is to live the faith. But this search for alternative realities—whether it takes the form of an eclectic religiosity, the belief in magic and the occult, the frequent use of psychedelics, or simply meditation exercises—is an almost universal characteristic both in the communes and in the counter culture in general.

In a seller's market where extravagant claims are being made for dozens of different paths to salvation and the unexplored realms beyond rationality, a congeries of species is admitted, the foolish and the merely superstitious along with the wise and the ecstatic. A glance at the books that are offered in any of the stores specializing in astrology and the occult illustrates the point. One, a popular book by Louise Huebner, the "official witch of Los Angeles," is called *Power Through Witchcraft*. The jacket copy supplies all the important details about the author: "Mrs. Huebner lives in Los Angeles in a haunted house surrounded by ancient trees. She is an Aries with Taurus rising, with her ruling planet Venus conjunct Uranus in the 12th house and the moon in Capricorn." Inevitably, there's something akin to mail-order mysticism, crash courses in psychic power. The Silva Mind Control Institute guarantees that after a four-day course, you'll be able to tap into the cosmic consciousness. Satisfaction guaranteed or your money back. And the so-called Jesus-Freaks started something that has already become a major industry. There is Jesus-Rock music, a handful of dramatic offerings like *Godspell* and *Jesus Christ Superstar*, Jesus shirts (JESUS IS MY LORD emblazoned across the front, available in three sizes and several different colors), and even a Jesus-People wristwatch. Obviously, there's money in the Messiah.

Much of this can be dismissed as a fad, as nothing more consequential than goldfish swallowing or Hula Hoops. But what are we to make of the rest of it? How much of this is a deliberate put-on, and how much a real search for the sacred? In a sense, the interest in this whole range of alternative realities is more important than whether they are "real," however *that* is to be determined. What religion, astrology, and the occult have in common is that they are ways of admitting to awareness forces that reason and a scientific world view reject out of hand. They are different ways of insisting that the universe is a far vaster place than our science, our logic, and our intelligence would lead us to believe, a way of protesting against the false claims that science has been making as the *only* valid form of knowledge. Even if those who are serious about their religious pursuits are outnumbered by those who are aimlessly rummaging about in the attic of mystic traditions, the rediscovery of the supernatural is a form of protest against "single vision and Newton's sleep," an attempt to find a larger vision of reality by trying out some of the *other* forms of human consciousness.

When three shrieking women dressed in tattered garments and pointed hats, representatives of WITCH (Women's International Terrorists Corps from Hell), put a hex on the sociology department at the University of Chicago not long ago, they combined high comedy with an earnest protest against the narrow reality that the social sciences recognize. It is difficult to describe the event without sliding off into parody which overlooks the fact that there *was* a serious message. Any excursion into alternative realities is laughable from the point of view of normal everyday consciousness because it violates the assumptions built into that world view. But to miss the seriousness of this quest for the supernatural is to miss an important part of the meaning of the counter culture.[1]

Who would have guessed five years ago that there would be a religious explosion, especially among the middle-class young? Who would have predicted that refugees from affluent families would be scouring the countryside for fresh religious traditions, finally to adopt those of the American Indian? And who would have anticipated that rebellious teenagers would be carrying hip-pocket Bibles, chastizing their parents with Scriptural quotations, and causing the ultimate embarrassment of using Christian literature to condemn the churches for diluting the faith?

Despite the fact that about four out of ten Americans, and about half of the nation's college population, still goes to church every weekend, surveys taken during the last decade indicate that most people believe that religion has been losing its influence on American life.[2] In many quarters the demise of the supernatural has been a foregone conclusion for some time now. Secularization appeared to be an almost inevitable and irreversible trend in modern civilization. It was assumed that the gods had been cast out, that in a society no longer dominated by religious symbols and institutions, God was in fact something of an anachronism. Secularization denotes the declining influence of the church, as in our modern insistence on the separation of church and state. But more importantly, secularization refers to something that goes on in our heads: We no longer understand the meaning of everyday life in terms of symbols and concepts laden with religious significance. The most popular theological writings of the mid-sixties announced the "death of God." Almost every theologian had a different interpretation of its meaning, but most of those who proclaimed the death of God agreed that attention should be shifted from a transcendent, supernatural God "out there" to the secular life in human society. Harvey Cox declared that "the era of metaphysics is dead," and that "politics replaces metaphysics as the language of theology."

Like Freud, contending that religion is fundamentally an illusion, something that mankind has to get over when it finally comes of age, the modern tendency is to write off religion as a dispensable element in human society, as if we could do without the systems of meanings that it has provided.

Alan Watts once commented that the socially approved version of reality is "more or less the world as perceived on a bleak Monday morning," deprived of awe, ecstasy, or fantasy. What has happened in the church, the institutional agent that has traditionally been responsible for alternative realities, is that dreary Sunday-morning services increasingly reflect the bleak reality of Monday morning. Throughout history, as Peter Berger has aptly put it, religion has been "in the ecstasy business almost by definition." [3] The essence of any religious system is its contention that there is another realm than that of everyday experience, a realm of ultimate significance for man. The primary function of religious systems has been to explain the complex ways in which that other world is related to this one. But in this secular era the churches provide no alternative reality. This is one of the reasons why the latter-day believers in the counter culture reject organized religion, especially Protestantism: It accepts the same one-dimensional version of man that is assumed by the society in general. It is very natural in a society so firmly committed to the cognitive universe of science that the churches should have withdrawn from the "ecstasy business." But by doing so they abdicate their responsibility for providing an alternative way of looking at the world and an alternative form of consciousness, and provide instead just a Sunday supplement to everyday reality.

A number of people with firmly established credentials in the normal mode of consciousness have insisted that there are realms that positivism leaves completely untouched. Writing of his experience with mescaline, Aldous Huxley spoke in *The Doors of Perception* of "the urge to transcend self-conscious selfhood as a principal appetite of the soul," and the need "to be shaken out of the ruts of ordinary perception, to be shown for a few timeless hours the outer and the inner world, not as they appear to an animal obsessed with survival or to a human being obsessed with words and notions, but as they are apprehended, directly and unconditionally by Mind at Large." Huxley suggested that the human brain and nervous system act as a "reducing valve," that we have traded in Mind at Large, which understands the unity of the universe, for a selective perception, an awareness reduced to that kind of practical consciousness that makes biological survival possible. "Most people, most of the time, know only what comes through the reducing valve and is consecrated as genuinely real by the local language. Certain persons, however, seem to be born with a kind of by-pass that circumvents the reducing valve. In others, temporary by-passes may be acquired either spontaneously, or as the results of deliberate 'spiritual exercises,' or through hypnosis, or by means of drugs." By these means, some people experience a universe "different from the carefully selected utilitarian material which our narrowed, individual minds regard as a complete, or at least sufficient picture of reality."

Fifty years earlier, in what is probably the most frequently quoted passage from *The Varieties of Religious*

Experience, William James defended the mystic states of consciousness which even then were in disrepute:

> . . . our normal waking consciousness, rational consciousness as we call it, is but one special type of consciousness, whilst all about it, parted from it by the filmiest of screens, there lie potential forms of consciousness entirely different. We may go through life without suspecting their existence; but apply the requisite stimulus, and at a touch they are there in their completeness. . . . No account of the universe can be final which leaves these other forms of consciousness quite disregarded. How to regard them is the question—for they are so discontinuous with ordinary consciousness. Yet they may determine attitudes though they cannot furnish formulas, and open a region though they fail to give a map. At any rate, they forbid a premature closing of our accounts with reality. Looking back on my own experiences, they all converge toward a kind of insight to which I cannot help ascribing some kind of metaphysical significance.

These other forms of consciousness may indeed have metaphysical significance, but the cast of religious geniuses which James assembles in this volume—those people who specialize in altered states of consciousness—would hardly be welcome in this society. It has always been much easier to live with mystics in history books, where they are presented as the founders of religious systems, than to live with them as contemporaries. There is an almost inevitable clash between those who take other realities seriously and the guardians of the everyday reality. In a one-dimensional society, the only recognized vocabulary for talking about these excursions into other forms of consciousness is that of psychiatry. From the point of view of psychiatry, a good deal of what goes on in the communes where religion is taken quite seriously would be labeled as madness. Here, for example, is Mel Lyman, the leader of Boston's Fort Hill Community, introducing himself in the community paper, the *Avatar:* "To those of you who are unfamiliar with me, let me introduce myself by saying that I am truth and I speak the truth. . . . In all humility I tell you that I am the greatest man in the world and it doesn't trouble me in the least." In another issue of the *Avatar,* these words accompany his picture: "I'm Christ, I swear to God in PERSON, and I'm about to turn this foolish world upside down."

The problem is clear enough. The clash between the counter culture and the mainstream culture is in one of its aspects the clash between two fundamentally different ways of looking at the world. The counter culture recognizes the reality of the unseen and the authority of experiences for which there is no "evidence" acceptable to science. As James put it, the problem with mystic states is that they are "so discontinuous with ordinary consciousness." It is easy enough to hope for some kind of synthesis of these two perspectives, a widening of our visions to allow *both* kinds of experience. Yet the two perspectives are so radically incompatible that I doubt whether any such mutual recognition will soon take place. There are very effective means of enforcing the ratified one-dimensional version of reality, and none so harsh as the label of madness.

Socrates commented in the *Phaedrus* that our greatest blessings come to us through madness, provided that the madness comes from God. The significance of the point, that going mad may be the ultimate form of illumination, hasn't been lost on the counter culture. *Howl,* one of its founding documents, was dedicated to a mental patient.

Timothy Leary wasn't advocating madness when he said that "it becomes necessary for us to go out of our minds in order to use our heads." [4] He was, rather, in his favorite role as the Pied Piper of the psychedelic movement, expressing the belief that it is through ecstatic experience rather than the use of intellect that we most fully use our heads. The agent that Leary has so conspicuously advocated for those trips is, of course, LSD. Any attempt to account for the counter culture's fascination with alternative realities has to begin with the psychedelics, which were largely responsible for opening up new inner vistas for so many young people. So much of what has been said about the psychedelics—both pro and con—has been either hysterical, ill-informed, or dangerously dogmatic that I hesitate even to enter the discussion. There is almost nothing that can be said about them without elaborate qualifications. And yet, finally, there is no way of accounting for many of the characteristics of the counter culture without admitting their importance. Next to the "drug problem," sex looks like a melodramatic exaggeration we invented way back when to keep life interesting during some pretty routine times. It is, to a considerable extent, the psychedelics and the changes which they triggered that make this generation different from the preceding ones and color every part of this new variety of radicalism.

Most of the discussions about psychedelics, like the innumerable conferences on the subject, are fractured between those who have already had the experience (and speak ex cathedra from the authority of their own vision) and those who haven't and won't (but still feel qualified to pass judgment on it). On the one hand, the true believers. On the other, the objective observers.

To the true believers, the psychedelic experience gains its authority from the fact that it is more real than ordinary reality:

> My first psychedelic experience was triggered by 400 milligrams of mescalin sulfate. It did induce a flight, but instead of fleeing from reality, I flew more deeply into it. I had never before seen, touched, heard, smelled, and felt so profound a personal unity and involvement with the concrete material world. . . . My exponentially heightened awareness saw through the static, one-dimensional, ego-constructed false front which is the consciousness-constructed reality of the everyday world. This was no evasive flight from, but a deep probe into reality.[5]

That the psychedelic-induced vision takes on authority as an insight into what reality *really* is, and that, as a consequence, the person's future actions will be shaped by this experience—these are signals that there is a social as well as a psychological and a medical issue at stake here.

To the objective observer, such affirmations of a reality more real than everyday reality are a clear sign of some sort of temporary psychotic state. In response to the true believers' contention that these visions have some sort of religious significance, the skeptics answer that those who take drugs grasp the vocabulary of religion as a convenient metaphor for this state of derangement. After all, what does it mean to insist that you "understand everything," that "you feel a profound sense of personal unity with the concrete material world"? And anyway, the skeptics ask, how could anything genuinely spiritual come out of a tab of mescaline or a sugar cube soaked with LSD? What does religion mean if we can gain entrance into the mystic beyond without doing our spiritual exercises and paying our dues? And then the critics haul out the medical arguments: Don't the psychedelics turn minds into oatmeal? Don't they cause uncontrollable flashbacks? Don't they lead to a life of drug dependency? . . .

Here we enter a swamp of controversy that I have neither the space nor the medical knowledge to get us out of. The best that I can do is to offer a few impressionistic comments and to suggest what sort of problem I think the "drug problem" really is.

Even if there is no evidence that the psychedelics are addictive, it is clear that for some people they do lead to destructive forms of habituation. The grim fact of adolescent trippers taking a tab a day in order to keep reality at a distance should be enough to convince people that the better part of responsibility in the matter is not to legalize all forms of psychedelics and make them as readily available as bubble gum and candy bars. But neither is it to ban their use entirely, to make them all illegal. The selective use of psychedelics as a medicine or a religious sacrament, rather than a form of entertainment, makes very good sense. Alan Watts has pointed out that we are very willing to use a strong medicine in order to cure a serious disease, even when we're not quite sure what the side effects of that medicine may be. Our narrowed sense of reality may be such a serious disease. We don't condemn the use of strong medicine because it may be harmful if taken as a steady diet; it seems to me that the same attitude would be appropriate with regard to the psychedelics. Of course this leads to the thorny question of access: Who's going to be responsible for dispensing the psychedelics? Who's going to be elibigle to use them, and for what purposes? A psychedelic pharmacy obviously poses much knottier problems than the ordinary street-corner variety.

Many of these problems are solved by regarding psychedelics as a sacrament, as the peyote religion does, and limiting their use to religious ceremonies. A sacrament is the outward sign of an inward grace, an agent that cleanses and brings new life. The psychedelics are well suited to the role. Judging from some of the recent evidence, they may have played a much larger role in the history of world religion than many of us suspected, and certainly a more important role than any of the established churches would be willing to admit.[6] The care with which peyote is used in the ritual of the Native American Church (which is the official name of the peyote religion) is a way of recognizing and respecting its power. And there is no better form of group therapy to prevent "bad trips" than to be surrounded by a small congregation of fellow believers in an atmosphere of trust and love.

It is true that all the medical facts about the various psychedelic agents aren't yet in. But neither are all the facts in about most of what we consume, most conspicuously many of the medically approved drugs. The fact that many more people express concern about the medical effects of the psychedelics than about the medically approved drugs seems to me a suspicious case of selective attention, an indication of what really bothers most people about the psychedelics. What would happen if a biochemist devised a way to make all the psychedelics medically harmless? What would happen if it were discovered that they already were? It would certainly not be a solution to the "drug problem." The problem has more to do with the social implications of drug use than with their medical effects. To clinch what is fundamentally a moral argument with a medical warning is to sidestep the issue. Both cigarettes and alcohol are bad for us, but they pose no threat to our civilization. But the act of drug taking is now one of the most popular ways of seceding from this civilization, opting out of the ordinary universe of assumptions, obligations, and responsibilities.

Irving Kristol recently compared the widespread apprehension about drug use with the way alcohol was feared a century ago. Many people agreed then that alcohol posed a real social threat. It was being used by the new working classes in such a way as to impede their assimilation into bourgeois society. In marked contrast to most of the contemporary critics of psychedelics, those who led the Prohibition movement offered both medical and moral arguments. They answered the subversive question "Why *not* take alcohol?" with a list of moral traits considered to be desirable among self-reliant citizens in an urban society. As Kristol points out, when drug takers ask the question "Why not?" those who oppose their use seem incapable of answering the question and resort instead to medical arguments.[7] The reason why the "drug problem" is such a huge problem is that it calls into question many of the basic features of our society and many of the assumptions which are most firmly embedded in our heads.

Those inner vistas that were opened up by the psychedelics are now being explored by a variety of different paths. The "God thirst" which many young people experience demonstrates the truth of Leary's assertion that the most potent power of the psychedelics is to arouse "latent religious sensitivities." Whether or not Leary would approve, many of the religious faiths to which young people are now turning strenuously oppose the use of *any* chemical agents. Meher Baba, considered by many to be an avatar, one of the most spiritually realized men of this age, leaves no doubt about how he feels about LSD and the other psychedelics:

> LSD is said to expand consciousness and alter one's personality for the better. In America, it has become tragically popular among the young, used indiscriminately by any and many. They must be persuaded to desist from taking drugs, for they are harmful—physically, mentally, and spiritually. . . .
>
> No drug, whatever its greatest promises, can help to attain the spiritual goal. There is no short-cut to the goal except through the grace of the Perfect

Master, and drugs, LSD more than others, gives only a semblance of "spiritual experience," a glimpse of a false reality.[8]

Meher Baba is by no means the only one counseling people to stay away from drugs. One of the wandering Jesus-Freaks I encountered near Big Sur, a gospel-spreading believer bearing on his arm a large tattoo of Christ wearing a crown of thorns, had the same idea: "You don't need any pills, that's the far-out thing. Just drop a little Matthew, Mark, Luke, and John. Christ is the ultimate trip."

No matter how people get their insights, the one thing the new religions have in common is that they carry almost no resemblance to the established forms of religion —Sunday-morning services, church bazaars, and Christmas pageants—which many of these young people grew up with. Like so many of the other characteristics of the counter culture, its religious practices, borrowed from East and West, seem an absolutely haphazard collection. There are large numbers of young people among the ranks of the Jesus-Freaks, but also a large number of adherents to the peyote religion and an assortment of Zen-inspired meditational religions. The attraction of the religions of Asia is probably that they have no rigid conceptualization of God and that they offer words and images that are fresh, untainted by long contact with stale religious practices. Although Christianity offers the example of Jesus as fellow martyr to the cause of peace and brotherhood, it is harder to understand its appeal, loaded as it is with such associations.

For all the proselytizing of some of the Jesus-Freaks, young people of different religious persuasions coexist and respect one another's beliefs with little regard for doctrinal or sacramental differences. Many of them borrow from two or three different traditions. I remember one girl carrying a knapsack on which pictures of Jesus and Yogananda's guru had been sewn who was enthusiastically rapping about Sufism while leafing through a tattered copy of *The Aquarian Gospel*. Perhaps there is a fairly obvious explanation for this eclectic religiosity. The emphasis in almost all of the religious practices that have been adopted by the young is on developing each person's awareness of the Godhead, on heightening the visionary experience. In the anti-organizational climate of the counter culture, the church—which represents a codified system of beliefs and practices while it acts as an intermediary between man and God—is rejected. Religious heroes are regarded not as the founders of religious systems, but as gurus. Thus Buddha, Jesus, and Yogananda's guru can all be admired and emulated as men who have attained a particularly high level of spiritual development.

Predictably, in this climate where so many unfamiliar forms of religiosity are being tested, the guardians of the status quo have been most reluctant to give them official recognition. One of these new cults, the Neo-American Church, attempted to follow the precedent of the peyote religion by claiming that LSD and marijuana are used as sacraments in its ceremony. Mrs. Judith Kuch, a twenty-five-year-old minister of the church, asked the U.S. District Court to dismiss an indictment against her for illegal drug possession, contending that her right to the free exercise of religious beliefs had been violated. The judge refused to dismiss the indictment. He said that after reading the "so-called catechism and handbook of the church . . . one gains the inescapable impression that the membership is mocking established institutions, playing with words, and is totally irreverent in any sense of the term." The judge pointed out that the church symbol is a three-eyed toad, that its official songs are "Puff, the Magic Dragon," and "Row, Row, Row Your Boat." Since the religious experience itself admits of no test, the judge concluded on the basis of available evidence that a church consisting of such "goofy nonsense" could not be a legally recognized religion.[9]

In this program of mining the most valuable ideas that are represented in the youth communes, my emphasis in this chapter has been on the positive and necessary task of enlarging our conception of reality. Obviously there is another aspect—a negative and escapist one—to this search for alternative realities. The attraction to the occult and the irrational often signals the abandonment of the critical faculties, an attack on reason which is a dangerous development in the youth culture. For many of those who followed Leary on his ecstatic trip, psychedelics offer nothing more than a flight from responsibility and an excuse for total withdrawal.

Many of the discussions of the counter culture emphasize its rejection of rationality without noticing the other, more positive aspects of this search for alternative realities. Nearly every society has some sort of moratorium for young people, a period during which its members are allowed to try out different roles before coming of age and committing themselves to some particular style of adulthood. In Erik Erikson's words, the moratorium is "a time for horse stealing and vision-quests, a time for Wanderschaft or work 'out West' or 'down under,' a time for 'lost youth' or academic youth, a time for self-sacrifice or for pranks—and today, often a time for patienthood or delinquency." Each new generation must ask the why and what for questions and find answers that are meaningful in its own era. In historical eras such as this one, when the "solutions" of the parents' generation are largely irrelevant to the experience of the younger generation, the process of coming to an identity is almost inevitably difficult. The potential of youth in this process of psychosocial evolution, as Erikson put it, is to act as "renewers of its ethical strength, as rebels bent on the destruction of the outlived." [10] And also as innovators testing new cultural alternatives. The communes are something more than a place for a youthful moratorium (although it remains to be seen whether they will become real communities, the units of an alternative society), but much of what goes on in them is understandable in these terms. Because of the prevailing attitudes in most of the groups as well as their physical isolation, they provide a miniature society which is almost uniquely insulated against the mainstream society, thereby providing a nearly ideal setting for a moratorium.

In many societies, the moratorium includes something like the "vision-quest" of the Plains Indians.[11] Before coming of age, the boys in many of the Plains tribes were expected to go on a solitary search, and through fasting, self-torture, or the use of hallucinogens to invite visionary experiences. Returning to their tribes, they were respected for their new powers. The visionary experience then became the central fact in their religious practice as an adult. In a curious way, the communes provide the setting for a new kind of vision-quest. They are a place for getting out of one's head in a society that rejects all sorts of visionary experiences.

In exploring these alternative forms of consciousness the young may be recovering a latent possibility for the rest of the society. "There comes a time—I believe we are in such a time—" said Norman O. Brown, "when civilization has to be renewed by the discovery of new mysteries." [12] This sense of awe and respect for a universe much vaster than that described by science has been expressed by people of much more wisdom and experience than the youthful rebels. This is how Albert Einstein spoke of it:

The most beautiful thing we can experience is the mysterious. It is the source of all true art and science. He to whom this emotion is a stranger, who can no longer pause to wonder and stand rapt in awe, is as good as dead: his eyes are closed. This insight into the mystery of life, coupled though it be with fear, has also given rise to religion. To know that what is impenetrable to us really exists, manifesting itself as the highest wisdom and the most radiant beauty which our dull faculties can comprehend only in their most primitive form—this knowledge, this feeling, is at the center of true religiousness.[13]

"To know that what is impenetrable to us really exists. . . ." At its best, it is this awareness which we have to gain from the search for alternative realities.

10 : Thesis, Antithesis . . . Synthesis?

> . . . no longer is it merely for the old to teach the young the meaning of life, whether individual or collective. It is the young who, by their responses and actions, tell the old whether life as represented by the old and presented to the young has meaning; and it is the young who carry in them the power to confirm those who confirm them, and joining the issues, to renew and to regenerate, or to reform and to rebel.
>
> —Erik Erikson

"The revolution of the twentieth century will take place in the United States," declares Jean-Francois Revel. "It is only there that it can happen. And it has already begun." [1] What kind of revolution is this? Charles Reich tells us that it "will originate with the individual and with culture, and it will change the political structure only as its final act. It will not require violence to succeed, and it cannot be successfully resisted by violence. It is now spreading with amazing rapidity. . . . It is both necessary and inevitable, and in time it will include not only youth, but all people in America." [2]

As in all turbulent times, there are other prophets with different messages. Far from assuming, as Reich does, that these drop-outs from the affluent society who are populating the communes are the wave of the future, Peter Drucker suggests just the opposite: "To me, it seems far more probable that during the Seventies this country will return to a preoccupation with the traditional economic worries. Indeed, during the next decade economic performance—with jobs, savings, and profits at the center—may well become more important than it was in the Sixties." [3] Drucker looks at some characteristics of the American population, especially at the fact that the youth revolt is manned by the products of the postwar baby boom. Had anyone bothered a decade ago, he says, to notice that the center of gravity of the American population would shift dramatically in the sixties all the way down to age seventeen and to anticipate the psychological consequences of that shift, he could have predicted this revolt. As the social tenor of the sixties was in part a consequence of the baby boom, Drucker argues that the tenor of the seventies can be predicted by anticipating the consequences of the "baby bust" that followed. One sure fact, he says, is that seventeen-year-olds, who are "rebellious, in search of a new identity, and intoxicated with new ideas," grow up to be young adults, who tend to be quite conventional, concerned with "the prosaic details of grubby materialism." Add to this the fact that there is likely to be a scarcity of jobs for college graduates in the 1970's, and you get a very different kind of prophecy for the coming decade from that of Revel or Reich. "It is just conceivable that the 19-year-old hard-hat— precisely because he is already exposed to the realities of economic life which are soon to shock college graduates —prefigures the values, the attitudes, and the concerns to which today's rebellious youths will switch tomorrow. . . . The graduates from today's youth culture are likely to find themselves far more worried about jobs and money than they now suspect." Drucker concludes that "in the issues that matter to them, in their values and, above all, in their needs, the Seventies may be a very traditional—indeed, a quite old-fashioned—decade." [3]

Even for turbulent times, these are extraordinarily different prophecies. Yet the main lines of argument about the counter culture and its revolutionary potential lead to conclusions that are just as radically at odds with each other as are these two positions. One group of analysts takes a counterrevolutionary view of the youth revolt. To their way of thinking, the youthful rebels who are turning away from their middle-class pasts and striking out against intellect, technology, and large-scale organization are engaged in a revolt which is foredoomed. Historical momentum as well as political power is on the side of the emerging post-industrial society, which has little sympathy for "obsolete" ideas such as anarchism, consciousness expansion, and liberation. Another group of social analysts assumes that youth is indeed a revolutionary force. Reich's *The Greening of America* is one example of this kind of argument, which takes a substantially different form in the writings of Theodore Roszak, Philip Slater, or any of a dozen other sympathetic accounts of the youth culture. The common belief—one that I share and have discussed in the early chapters of this book—is that the success of industrial civilization has in large part rendered the assumption of scarcity obsolete. As a consequence, both the mental habits and the life style appropriate to an era of scarcity can be, and in fact should be, replaced. Most of these analysts emphasize, as I have, what the counter culture has to offer at its best: a vision of a different and better society.

There is a striking difference not just in the conclusions to which these two lines of argument lead, but also the kind of analysis upon which they depend. As Kenneth Keniston has pointed out in a very useful discussion of the debate, those who take the counterrevolutionary position offer an analysis of social institutions, the mode of production, and the formal organization of roles and relationships.[4] Or, like Drucker, they base their conclusions on the size and structure of the population. As opposed to this social-structural analysis, those who assume the revolutionary potential of the youth culture focus on change at the cultural level. Their emphasis is on new value systems and new forms of consciousness.

As Keniston remarks, each of these approaches neglects what the other stresses. As a consequence neither, taken alone, is entirely adequate as a way of understanding the counter culture and its revolutionary potential. Those who assume that the counter culture is a revolutionary force tend to overlook the fact that social institutions are not just a derivative of cultural facts, that ideals and aspirations—indeed, our whole symbolic apparatus—are influenced in many different ways by the institutional framework. Those who deny the revolutionary potential of the youth culture, those whose analysis stresses social-structural factors, commit what I think is an even more serious mistake. They overlook the possibility that we may be witnessing a crisis in belief systems, a civilizational systems break. The conflict of allegiances which the clash between the mainstream culture and the counter culture represents runs much deeper than the issues that divided the country in the early sixties. What is at stake are many of the values and assumptions that are the foundations of industrial civilization.

The question is simple enough, even if the answer is not: What are the prospects for this youthful oppositional culture, created by a generation which *Fortune* called "the most interesting to come along in U.S. history"? What is its revolutionary potential? And what is likely to happen to the rural communes, these scattered outposts of what is advertised as the emerging alternative society? One thing is clear. This is not the revolution that Marx forecast, in which the opponents were to line up according to their class affiliations and the proletariat was to wrest power from the capitalist managers. Much of what I have said in earlier chapters should illustrate the point: This is indeed a *counter* culture, not just different from the mainstream culture but in many ways fundamentally opposed to it. But rather than the class alliances that Marx anticipated, most of the unique features of this revolt are a consequence of the fact that it represents a rejection of middle-class culture by the children of the middle class. Many children of the working classes, rather than attacking the citadels of economic power, are waiting in the wings, preparing to man the high-paying posts which are being abandoned by downwardly mobile middle-class drop-outs.[5]

Not primarily a political rebellion, this is now mainly an attack on the ratified values of an industrial, middle-class society. The trajectory of the movement during the last decade indicates that it is becoming less political than it was. Much of the evidence supports Reich's assertion that this rebellion originates "with the individual and with culture, and it will change the political structure only as its final act." In many respects, the strength of this revolt is that it is not political. It is essentially, in Rudi Dutschke's words, a "long march through all the institutions of the society." It is primarily an attack on the institutions that affect us most immediately, such as the family, and on the systems of allegiance which tie us to the status quo. If this attack seems futile, it is well to remember that institutions are never quite as impregnable and unalterable as they seem. One of the chief reasons for social stability is that the institutions which frame our everyday life fix themselves in our imagination; in ordinary circumstances the alternatives are almost unthinkable. And yet there are breaking points at which institutions are as irreversibly transformed as was the

Catholic Church during the Reformation or the European aristocracy after 1789. It is not inconceivable that the most taken-for-granted features of modern life, such as the nuclear family, or apparently fixed values and allegiances, might now be in the process of radical transformation.

The strength of the counter culture lies largely in the fact that its critique of American culture strikes at some of its weakest points—the huge investment of time, effort, and psyche in material possessions, the lack of community, and the unquestioned acceptance of "the bigger, the better" thinking. To the extent that the themes of this revolt overlap with a widespread dissatisfaction with American culture, the counter culture attracts the most unlikely assortment of allies and defenders. If it didn't happen every day, surely we would think that one of the most bizarre aspects of this potentially revolutionary situation is that reporters write sympathetic accounts of the voluntary primitivism of youth communes from their carpeted thirty-fourth floor offices in the Time-Life Building after expense-account luncheons at the Forum of the Twelve Caesars.

This youthful opposition is encouraged for a number of differing reasons, none so obvious as the insatiable hunger of the media for anything new or eccentric. Marx didn't anticipate anything quite so ironic as the fact that spokesmen for the most radical positions are paid handsomely for nation-wide network appearances in which they rail against the Establishment. The media welcome the opposition because its presence transforms even predetermined political rituals into good drama. How many people tuned in on the coverage of the 1968 Democratic Convention in Chicago because of anticipated Yippie atrocities, or because of reports that freaky-looking kids were handing shit sandwiches over the barricades to policemen, called pigs? What could be more natural than that the media—as officially designated voyeurs—would enthusiastically adopt the counter culture as a source of attractive escapist entertainment? Think, for example, of the appeal of the freedom portrayed in *Easy Rider* to people harnessed to nine-to-five jobs. Or of the attraction of the sexual freedom portrayed therein to people envious of any alternative to the monotony of monogamy.

There is another group, the Far Right, which needs the counter culture even more than the media do. If the hippies didn't exist, it would be necessary for the reactionary Right to invent them as the indispensable target for its tirades. It is a happy fact for the devoted Right-winger that, even more than the Commie, the hippie invites the charge that he is a disgrace not only to his country but to his sex.

In thinking about the future of this rebellion, it is important to remember that America provides exceptionally fertile soil for a certain kind of revolt. The conventional wisdom of young radicals about the suppression of dissent in Fascist Amerika notwithstanding, self-consciousness (which has often taken the form of self-accusation) as well as a tolerance of dissent and diversity have been characteristic of this country. An additional factor, the importance of which is difficult to overestimate, is that as a nation we value whatever is new and different. This trait determines our reaction to new ideas and social movements no less than our behavior in the marketplace. As opposed to Europe, which is so strongly influenced by the heavy hand of the past, America has always prided itself as a dynamic nation engaged in the process of self-transformation. Americans are much more likely to look to young people for new ideas and habits than are Europeans; this is one of the reasons for the unique influence of the youth culture in this country. It is also significant that a youth culture has a certain leverage that most oppositional forces don't enjoy. Specific manifestations of a youthful revolt can be suppressed fairly easily. But a generational revolt is very difficult to crush completely.

Yet when young radicals insist, as Tom Hayden did in *Trial,* on setting up "free territories" in such places as Berkeley, Isla Vista, Ann Arbor, rural Vermont, and the East Village, and then speak of these as "internal colonies" which will be "self-determined," he carries nonpolitical thinking to an extreme. This sort of statement has, I suppose, a certain rhetorical usefulness, but it overlooks the fact that these "free territories" are exceedingly vulnerable. The resentment of part of the older generation enraged by the mocking disrespect and open defiance of the young provides the fuel for a formidable backlash. Even among the rural communes hidden away in the hills of Oregon or Vermont, harassment by unsympathetic neighbors, who generally have the local police and other public agencies on their side, is a serious threat.

But an even more serious threat to the existence of these scattered hip settlements comes from within. Like the nineteenth-century communitarian experiments, they are very fragile and more often shattered by internal problems than external threats. In an article on student dissent in Italy, Nicola Chiaromonte suggested that the young radicals "must detach themselves, must become resolute 'heretics.' They must detach themselves quietly, without shouting or riots, indeed in silence and secrecy; not alone but in groups, in real 'societies' that will create, as far as possible, a life that is independent and wise. . . . It would be . . . a non-rhetorical form of 'total rejection.' " [6] This, of course, is what has happened in the communal revolt in this country. And yet what an extrordinarily difficult task it is to construct a community in which life is "independent and wise." Traveling around the country to different communes, I very often had the feeling that they were populated by the wrong people trying to do the right things. The young people in their late teens and early twenties who have taken on this ambitious task are very poorly prepared to succeed in it. If the best prophet of the future is the past, then most of these communes stand little chance of surviving.

Perhaps the most important function that the communes now serve is as a greenhouse for the new sensibility, as a place where young recruits are converted to the counter culture. In this sense, they serve as a potent agent for social change. Linked to the widespread use of psychedelics, which act as a catalyst for the new sensibility, the communes provide a consensual universe removed from the faith-eroding effects of the mainstream culture.

In many respects, the most important question is not whether the communes survive in their present form, but rather what will be the fate of the ideas that they transmit. The average life-span of the rural settlements is less significant than what their "graduates" choose to do when they leave. It is my impression that conversion to the values of the counter culture is a far less transient thing than analysts like Drucker assume. Some of the graduates of communal life may well cut their hair a bit shorter, but I doubt whether many will revert to an unswerving concern for what Drucker called "the prosaic details of grubby materialism."

This revolution is not at all inevitable, as Reich believes, but in many ways it is necessary. And yet any new idea that receives as little critical and sympathetic attention and as much derision and moral condemnation as the communes have is likely to wither.

"We now have the abnormal situation," said Paul Goodman, "that in the face of the extraordinary novelties and complexities of modern times, there is no persuasive program for social reconstruction, thought up by many minds, corrected by endless criticism, made practical by much political activity. . . . The young are honorable and see the problems, but they don't know anything because we have not taught them anything."[7] Even when they oscillate between total despair and visionary hope, the most beautiful characteristic of these young people is their vision of what is possible, their hope that a new and radically different social order can grow up in the midst of the technological society. To despair prematurely of the communes as desperate, adolescent ventures is to give up hope that there are any alternatives. Since in history as in nature there are as many new beginnings as dead ends, we have a responsibility to keep our minds open to fresh possibilities and untested alternatives.

Acknowledgments

Many of the ideas which I explore here grew out of discussions that I had several years ago with two extraordinary teachers, Helen Gregutt and Warren Ramshaw.

Special thanks to Daina Renard and also to Bill Bowman and Don Fersh for their help at various points. I might never have survived the hardest part of this work without the hospitality and encouragement of Claire Samstag.

Any book, I suppose, makes extravagant demands on the writer's time and energy. For sharing my enthusiasms and understanding my absences—both mental and physical—I have many friends to thank, especially Dina, Tom and Karen, Leslie, Peggy, and Larry and Karla.

Finally, many thanks to my brothers and sisters in communes across the country, who not only put up with me but encouraged me to put it together in words. I hope that what I've done does justice to what you've done.

Bibliographical Notes

In the notes that follow I have tried to acknowledge all of the writers who have influenced my thinking in this book. In particular, I am indebted to three authors whose influence is reflected in almost every chapter, Kenneth Keniston, Theodore Roszak, and Philip Slater.

Until recently, when communes started to receive a great deal of attention, many of the most valuable discussions of the communal movement appeared in underground journals that, unfortunately, are not very accessible. The four that I have found to be most useful are *The Modern Utopian, The Green Revolution, Alternate Society,* and *WIN Magazine.*

Preface

1. Peter Marin, "The Open Truth and Fiery Vehemence of Youth: A Sort of Soliloquy," p. 2 in Mitchell Goodman, ed., *The Movement Toward a New America* (New York: Alfred A. Knopf, 1970).

1: Introduction: The Uses of Utopia

1. Philip Slater, *The Pursuit of Loneliness* (Boston: Beacon Press, Inc., 1970).
2. Eric Hoffer, *The Ordeal of Change* (New York: Harper and Row, Publishers, 1967), p. 54.
3. Slater, p. 7.
4. Marvin Garson, "Crime, chrome, cream," *WIN Magazine,*

March 1, 1969, reprinted in Mitchell Goodman, ed., *The Movement Toward a New America*, p. 121.

5. Slater, p. 100.
6. San Francisco *Chronicle*, August 17, 1970, p. 14.
7. San Francisco *Oracle*, February, 1967, p. 3.
8. "The Family," *WIN Magazine*, January 1, 1969, n.p.
9. *The Modern Utopian*, Vol. IV, No. 2, Spring, 1970, n.p.
10. Quoted in Reuel Denney, "American Youth Today," in Erik Erikson (ed.), *The Challenge of Youth* (Garden City: Doubleday Anchor Books, 1965), p. 165.
11. Kenneth Keniston, *The Uncommitted* (New York: Dell Books, 1965), p. 327.
12. David Riesman, "Some Observations on Community Plans and Utopias," in *Individualism Reconsidered* (New York: The Free Press, 1954), p. 76.
13. Quoted in Michael Harrington, *The Accidental Century* (Baltimore: Penguin Books, Inc., 1966), p. 24.
14. Karl Mannheim, *Ideology and Utopia* (New York: Harcourt, Brace, 1936), p. 263.
15. William Sheppard, Jr. (ed.), "Towards Walden Two: Proceedings of the 1966 National Walden Two Conference" (Ann Arbor: Campus Publishers, 1966), n.p.

2: *"America Is a Utopia"*

Mircea Eliade concludes a discussion of the utopian mission of the Americas with a fascinating, if somehow improbable, explanation of this characteristically American trait: "What must be emphasized is that the certainty of the eschatological mission, and especially of attaining once again the perfection of early Christianity and restoring paradise to earth, is not likely to be forgotten easily. It is very probable that the behavior of the average American today, as well as the political and cultural ideology of the United States, still reflects the consciousness of the Puritan certitude of having been called to restore the earthly paradise." ("Paradise and Utopia," in *Utopia and Utopian Thought* [Boston: Houghton Mifflin Company, 1966], pp. 260–280).

For useful surveys of the communitarian movement, see Ralph Albertson's "Survey of Mutualistic Communes in 19th

Century America," in *Iowa Journal of History and Politics*,
October, 1936, pp. 375–445; and Frederick Bushee, "Communistic Societies in the United States," in *Political Science
Quarterly*, Vol. XX, December, 1905, pp. 625–664. A. E. Bestor
includes a checklist of communitarian experiments through the
1850's in his *Backwoods Utopias* (Philadelphia: University
of Pennsylvania Press, 1950).

1. Quoted in F. S. C. Northrup, *The Meeting of East and
   West* (New York: Collier Books, 1966), p. 66.
2. George Ripley, "Model Phalanx," *The Harbinger*, January
   16, 1847, p. 94.
3. Quoted in John Humphrey Noyes, *History of American
   Socialisms* (New York: Dover Publicaticns, Inc., 1966),
   p. 46.
4. Arthur E. Bestor, "Patent-Office Models of the Good
   Society," in *American Historical Review*, Vol. LVIII, No.
   3, April, 1953, pp. 505–526.
5. Bestor, *Backwoods Utopias* (Philadelphia: University of
   Pennsylvania Press, 1950), p. 12.
6. Mark Holloway, *Heavens on Earth* (New York: Dover
   Publications, Inc., 1966), p. 19.
7. Acts 2:44–46.
8. Quoted in Bestor, *Backwoods Utopias*, p. 63.
9. Lindsay Swift, *Brook Farm* (New York: The Macmillan
   Company, 1900), pp. 15–16.
10. Quoted in Bestor, *Backwoods Utopias*, p. 114.
11. Holloway, *Heavens on Earth*, p. 108.
12. Quoted in Vernon L. Parrington, *Main Currents in American Thought* (New York: Harcourt, Brace, and Co.,
    1930), Vol. II, p. 343.
13. Quoted in Charles Nordhoff, *The Communistic Societies
    of the United States* (New York: Schocken Books, Inc.,
    1965), p. 289.
14. Nordhoff, *The Communistic Societies of the United States*,
    p. 387.
15. Noyes, *History of American Socialisms*, pp. 648–649.
16. Quoted in Martin Buber, *Paths in Utopia* (Boston: Beacon
    Press, Inc., 1960), p. 75.
17. Noyes, *History of American Socialisms*, p. 646.

18. Noyes, *History of American Socialisms*, p. 653.
19. Maren Lockwood, "The Experimental Utopia in America," in Frank E. Manuel, ed., *Utopias and Utopian Thought* (Boston: Houghton Mifflin Company, 1966), p. 192.

3: *Beyond Politics*

A number of writers have commented on the tension between radical activists and hippies. See, for example, Theodore Roszak's *The Making of a Counter Culture* (New York: Doubleday & Company, Inc., 1969) and William Braden's *The Age of Aquarius* (Chicago: Quadrangle Books, Inc., 1970). There is no comprehensive history of the counter culture, but the following books and articles are useful in constructing one: On the Beatniks, see Lawrence Lipton's *The Holy Barbarians* (New York: Julian Messner, 1959). Richard Neville's *Play Power* includes a good discussion of the Yippies (London: Jonathan Cape, 1970). Of the more comprehensive accounts, three are especially useful: Jack Newfield's *A Prophetic Minority* (New York: New American Library, 1966); *The New Radicals*, an anthology edited by Paul Jacobs and Saul Landau (New York: Random House, Inc., 1966); and Carl Oglesby's "Notes on a Decade Ready for the Dustbin," originally published in the August-September, 1969, *Liberation*, and reprinted in *The Movement Toward a New America*, edited by Mitchell Goodman (New York: Alfred A. Knopf, Inc., 1970).
1. See Ray Mungo's account of the meeting in *Famous Long Ago* (Boston: Beacon Press, Inc., 1970).
2. Rick Margolies, "On Community Building," *Alternate Society*, September, 1970.
3. Paul Goodman, *The New Reformation* (New York: Random House, Inc., 1970), Chapter Four.
4. Jacobs and Landau, *The New Radicals*, pp. 163–164.
5. Study by Philip E. Jacob, quoted in Elting Morison (ed.), *The American Style* (New York: Harper and Brothers, 1958), p. 163.
6. Jacobs and Landau, *The New Radicals*, p. 61.
7. From the Situationists' pamphlet, "De la misère en milieu étudiant, considerée sous ses aspects économique, poli-

tique, sexuel, et notamment intellectuel, et de quelques moyens pour y remédier" ["The Wretched State of the Student, Considered in Its Economic, Political, Psychological, Sexual, and Particularly Intellectual Aspects, and Some Ways of Remedying It"], p. 32. The Yippie and the Situationist strategies are similar in many respects. Both result from the convergence of traditionally political influences and literary and artistic influences. The Situationists refer to themselves as Marxists, but they also quote Sade, Artaud, and a variety of other artists and literary figures. Both were influenced as much by the Marx brothers as by Karl Marx. More importantly, both have attempted to reject revolutionary ideology completely and have emphasized the importance of a revolution in daily life. On the Situationists, see Guy Debord's *La Société du Spectacle* (Paris: Buchet-Chastel, 1967), and Alfred Willener's comments in *The Action-Image of Society* (New York: Pantheon Books, 1970), Part III.

8. There is an interesting consistency in the recurrence of the apocalyptic theme whenever a sensibility such as the counter culture's becomes widespread. Without exaggerating the similarities, there are striking parallels to the "revolutionary millenarianism" of the period from the eleventh century to the sixteenth century, which Norman Cohn discusses in *The Pursuit of the Millennium* (New York: Oxford University Press, 1957). Cohn's thesis is that in specific social circumstances, mass uncertainty and anxiety are channeled into movements that combine revolutionary impulses with an outburst of quasi-religious salvationism. Specifically, he comments on the recurrence of anarcho-communist millenarian groups within a much wider revolt. "In each of these instances the mass insurrection itself was directed towards limited and realistic aims—yet in each instance the climate of mass insurrection fostered a special kind of millenarian group. As social tensions mounted and the revolt became nation-wide, there would appear, somewhere on the radical fringe, a *propheta* with his following of paupers, intent upon turning this one particular upheaval into the apocalyptic

battle, the final purification of the world" [p. 284]. Schenk
comments on the same phenomenon in his book *The
Mind of the European Romantics* (Garden City: Doubleday Anchor Books, 1969), p. 32. During the first half of
the nineteenth century, the Romantic foreboding of an
impending collapse of the civilization was very widely
shared. In quite a different setting, John Humphrey Noyes
prophesied in 1830 that the world would come to an end
in 1880.

9. The Detroit *Free Press* articles on the FSM ran February
1–7, 1970. The articles were written by *Free Press* writers
Philip Meyer and Michael Maidenberg. Quoted in William
Braden, *The Age of Aquarius* (Chicago: Quadrangle,
1970), p. 253.

10. James T. Carey, *The College Drug Scene* (Englewood
Cliffs, N.J.: Prentice-Hall, Inc., 1968).

11. Francis Rigney and L. Douglas Smith, *The Real Bohemia*
(New York: Basic Books, 1961), quoted in Jack Newfield:
A Prophetic Minority (New York: New American Library,
1966), p. 45.

12. Aside from *Famous Long Ago* and *Total Loss Farm* (New
York: E. P. Dutton & Co., Inc., 1971), see Mungo's article
"If Mr. Thoreau Calls . . . ," which appeared in the
Atlantic, May, 1970. Predictably, the underground reviews
of Mungo's books betray the activist-hippie tension. This
one, which appeared in *WIN Magazine* (August, 1970,
p. 26), was written by Allen Young and followed the John
Lennon-John Hoyland precedent. Young's response to
Famous Long Ago: "The time has passed for any American, especially a white American male, to devote his time
to raptures over the trees and flowers of Vermont (which
Mungo does frequently in this book). We have learned
too much already to find peace in such deliberate am-
nesia. . . . How can we find peace of mind while white
people are oppressing blacks or while men dominate
women?"

4: The New Immediacy

There have been many different perspectives on the new immediacy. Norman O. Brown's discussion of the ideal of enjoyment that is immediate and absolute appears in his well-known book, *Life Against Death* (Middletown, Connecticut: Wesleyan University Press, 1959). From a very different perspective, Richard Neville explores the significance of play as an essential ingredient in the international underground in *Play Power* (London: Jonathan Cape, 1970). My largest debt in this chapter is to John Passmore's very fine article "Paradise Now: The Logic of the New Mysticism," which appeared in *Tncounter*, November, 1970.

On the similarities between the Romantic sensibility and the counter culture, I suggest H. G. Schenk's excellent summary volume, *The Mind of the European Romantics* (Garden City: Doubleday Anchor Books, 1969). The best single source on the German Youth Movement is still Howard Becker's *German Youth: Bond or Free* (New York: Oxford University Press, 1946).

1. Quoted in William Hedgepeth and Dennis Stock, *The Alternative* (London: Collier-Macmillan, Ltd., 1970), p. 19.
2. Report in *School and Society*, November, 1969.
3. Jean Jacques Rousseau, "A Discourse on the Origin of Inequality," in *The Social Contract and Discourses*, trans. G. D. H. Cole (New York: Everyman's Library, 1950), p. 182.
4. See Riley Dunlap, "Radical and Conservative Student Activists: A Comparison of Family Backgrounds," *Pacific Sociological Review*, Summer, 1970, pp. 171–181.
5. On this point and also for a useful discussion of the "generation gap" question, see Seymour Martin Lipset and Earl Raab, "The Non-Generation Gap," *Commentary*, August, 1970, pp. 35–39.
6. The fifth of the series by the Knight Newspapers on the FSM participants. The articles appeared in the Detroit *Free Press* from Feb. 1–7, 1970.
7. Kenneth Keniston, *Young Radicals* (New York: Harcourt, Brace & World, Inc., 1968).

8. Quoted in Lipset and Raab, "The Non-Generation Gap." See also Richard Flacks's chapter, "Who Protests: The Social Bases of the Student Movement," in Julian Foster and Durward Long (eds.), *Protest! Student Activism in America* (New York: William Morrow and Company, Inc., 1970).

9. Lewis Feuer, *The Conflict of Generations* (New York: Basic Books, 1969), p. 115.

10. Hannah Arendt, *On Violence* (New York: Harcourt, Brace & World, 1970), p. 65.

11. See Bennett Berger's interesting discussion of this point, "The New Stage of American Man—Almost Endless Adolescence," *New York Times Magazine*, November 2, 1969, p. 30 *et passim*.

12. It is important not to think of suburbia as a monolithic social phenomenon. Most of the communal young come from the more affluent middle-class suburban homes; very few of them come from families which have recently arrived in the middle class. Accordingly, in this discussion I am speaking specifically of upper-middle-class suburbs, not lower-middle or working-class suburbia. Most of the writings on the suburban pathologies take the upper-middle suburbs as the *only* variety of the species. Two well-informed students of suburbia have dissented from this view. See Herbert Gans' *The Levittowners* (New York: Pantheon Books, 1967), and Bennett Berger's comments in "Suburbia and the American Dream," *Public Interest*, Winter, 1966, pp. 80–92.

13. J. R. Seeley, R. A. Sim, and E. W. Loosley, *Crestwood Heights* (New York: John Wiley & Sons, Inc., 1963), p. 64.

14. Seeley, Sim, and Loosley, *Crestwood Heights,* pp. 6–7.

15. Quoted in John Passmore, "Paradise Now," p. 6.

16. Francis X. Sutton, Seymour E. Harris, Carl Kaysen, and James Tobin, *The American Business Creed* (Cambridge: Harvard Univ. Press, 1956), pp. 257–259.

17. *Albuquerque Journal*, June 22, 1970, p. 13.

18. On this point, see also Chapter Six in Philip Slater's *The Pursuit of Loneliness* (Boston: Beacon Press, Inc., 1970). I am indebted to Dr. Arthur Vidich for a number of the

observations on the life style of suburbia which appear in this chapter.

19. *"Le renouvellement de la société ne dependit jamais d'une révolution purement politique. . . . Ce sont les religions qui renouvellent les peuples."* Quoted in Schenk, *The Mind of the European Romantics,* p. 28.

20. Quoted in Schenk, *The Mind of the European Romantics,* p. 7.

21. Quoted in Schenk, *The Mind of the European Romantics,* p. 4.

22. Quoted in Schenk, *The Mind of the European Romantics,* p. 24.

23. On the German Youth Movement, see Howard Becker's *German Youth: Bond or Free* and S. N. Eisenstadt's *From Generation to Generation* (New York: The Free Press, 1956).

24. Peter Pulzer: *The Rise of Religious Anti-Semitism in Europe* (New York: John Wiley, 1964), p. 310.

25. Quoted in Fritz Stern, *The Politics of Cultural Despair* (Berkeley: Univ. of Calif. Press, 1963), p. 36.

26. Frantz Fanon, *The Wretched of the Earth* (New York: Grove Press, 1968), p. 176.

27. Aldous Huxley, *The Doors of Perception* (New York: Harper and Row, Publishers, 1954), pp. 34–35.

28. Kenneth Keniston, *The Uncommitted* (New York: Dell Books, 1960), Chapter Twelve.

29. See Irving Louis Horowitz' *Radicalism and the Revolt Against Reason: The Social Theories of Georges Sorel* (Carbondale, Illinois: Southern Illinois University Press, 1961).

30. Joseph Berke, "The Free University of New York," in Joseph Berke (ed.), *Counter Culture: The Creation of an Alternative Society* (London: Peter Owen, 1969). This book is a good example of what happens most of the time when the counter culture talks about itself. As an attempt at explanation or self-analysis, most of the selections are remarkably uninformative and mindless. But as a reflection of what the counter culture *is,* it's quite useful.

31. Quoted in John Passmore, "Paradise Now," from Antonin

Artaud, *Le Theatre et son Double* (Paris: Gallimard, 1964), p. 133.

32. Irving Howe, "The New York Intellectuals," *Commentary*, October, 1968, p. 24.

5: *The Anarchist Response*

1. Theodor Hertzka, *Freeland* (New York: D. Appleton and Co., 1891), quoted in Glenn Negley and J. Max Patrick, *The Quest for Utopia* (New York: Schuman, 1952), p. 134.
2. This appears as the epigraph in George Kateb's *Utopia and Its Enemies* (New York: Free Press of Glencoe, 1963).
3. For example, see Joseph Wood Krutch's *The Measure of Man* (New York: Harcourt, Brace, 1954); Donald C. Williams' "The Social Scientist as Philosopher and King," *Philosophical Review*, LVIII, 1949, pp. 345–359; Andrew Hacker's "The Spectre of Predictable Man," *The Antioch Review*, Vol. XIV, 1954, pp. 195–207; and John H. Bunzel's *Anti-Politics in America* (New York: Vintage Books, Inc., 1970), Chapter Six.
4. B. F. Skinner, "Some Issues Concerning the Control of Human Behavior," *Science*, CXXIV, 1956, p. 1059.
5. See Richard Todd's article " 'Walden Two,' Three? Many More?," *New York Times Magazine*, March 15, 1970, p. 24 *et passim*.
6. Skinner, "Some Issues Concerning the Control of Human Behavior," p. 1059.
7. Quoted in Isaac Deutscher, *Heretics and Renegades* (Indianapolis: The Bobbs-Merrill Company, Inc., 1969), p. 38.
8. Aldous Huxley, *Brave New World* (London: Chatto & Windus, 1932), p. 163.
9. Quoted in Marie Louise Berneri, *Journey Through Utopia* (London: Routledge and Kegan Paul, Ltd., 1950), p. 309. This is an excellent survey of utopian thought from ancient Greece to the present which emphasizes the authoritarian and intolerant nature of most of those visions.
10. Quoted in D. Novak, "The Place of Anarchism in the History of Political Thought," *The Review of Politics*, XX:3, July, 1958, pp. 307–320.

11. Quoted in Howard Zinn's introduction to Herbert Read's *Anarchy and Order* (Boston: Beacon Press, Inc., 1971), p. xviii.
12. Lewis Yablonsky, *The Hippie Trip* (New York: Pegasus Press, 1968), p. 47.
13. For discussions of the anarchist style in communes, see Benjamin Zablocki's *The Joyous Community* (New York: Penguin Books, Inc., 1971), Chapter Seven; and of earlier anarchist communities, Charles Gide's *Communist and Cooperative Colonies* (New York: Thomas Y. Crowell Co., n.d), Chapter Eight.
14. Alan Watts, "Beat Zen, Square Zen, Zen," in Watts' *This is It* (New York: The Macmillan Company, 1967), pp. 82–110.
15. See Theodore Roszak's comments in *The Making of a Counter Culture* (Garden City: Doubleday & Company, Inc., 1968), Chapter Four.
16. Richard Sennett's *The Uses of Disorder* (New York: Alfred A. Knopf, Inc., 1970) draws upon the anarchist tradition in a very original and important discussion of how city life might become richer and more life-affirming.

6: Gathering Together

1. Joy, "(To Sociologists and Publicists of the Beat Generation)," *Beatitude*, No. 8, August 15, 1959, n.p.

7: Individualism and Collectivism

Among the general discussions that relate to this chapter's themes, I especially recommend the following: Robert Nisbet's superb book *Community and Power* (London: Oxford University Press, 1953), Richard Sennett's *The Uses of Disorder* (New York: Alfred A. Knopf, Inc., 1971), and Philip Slater's *The Pursuit of Loneliness* (Boston: Beacon Press, Inc., 1970).

1. Peter Laslett, "The World We Have Lost," in Eric and Mary Josephson (eds.), *Man Alone* (New York: Dell Books, 1962).
2. Gary Snyder, "Why Tribe," in *Earth House Hold* (New York: New Directions, 1957), p. 113.

3. Martin Buber, *Paths in Utopia* (Boston: Beacon Press, Inc., 1949), p. 14.
4. Friedrich Nietzsche, *The Birth of Tragedy,* in *The Philosophy of Nietzsche* (New York: Modern Library, 1927), p. 956.
5. Morton Grodzins, *The Loyal and the Disloyal* (Chicago: The University of Chicago Press, 1956), pp. 238-242.
6. Harvey Cox, *The Secular City* (New York: The Macmillan Company, 1965).
7. Philippe Ariès, *Centuries of Childhood* (New York: Vintage Books, Inc., 1962).
8. Jacob Burckhardt, *The Civilization of the Renaissance in Italy* (London: Phaidon Press, 1950), p. 81.
9. On this point see, for example, Alfred Mirande, "The Isolated Nuclear Family Hypothesis: A Reanalysis," in John Edwards (ed.), *The Family and Change* (New York: Alfred A. Knopf, Inc., 1969), pp. 153-163.
10. Lloyd Warner and James C. Abegglen, *Big Business Leaders in America* (New York: Harper, 1955), p. 62.
11. William H. Whyte, Jr.: *The Organization Man* (New York: Doubleday Anchor Books, 1957), p. 314.
12. Archibald MacLeish, "Loyalty and Freedom," *American Scholar,* Autumn, 1953, p. 398.
13. Alexis de Tocqueville, *Democracy in America* (New York: Mentor, 1956), p. 192.
14. Dwight Macdonald, *Against the American Grain* (New York: Random House, Inc., 1952), p. 11.
15. Edward T. Hall, *The Hidden Dimension* (New York: Doubleday & Company, Inc., 1966).
16. Alan Watts, "A Psychedelic Experience: Fact or Fantasy?" in David Solomon (ed.), *LSD: The Consciousness-Expanding Drug* (New York: G. P. Putnam's Sons, 1966), p. 129.
17. Watts, in Solomon, p. 128.
18. Alan Watts, *The Joyous Cosmology* (New York: Vintage Books, Inc., 1962), pp. 18, 45.
19. Quoted in Nisbet, *Community and Power,* p. 61.

20. See, for example, Melford Spiro's account in *Kibbutz* (New York: Schocken Books, Inc., 1956).
21. Buber, *Paths in Utopia*, p. 135.
22. *Difficult But Possible Supplement to Whole Earth Catalog*, September, 1969, p. 23.
23. See Zablocki, *The Joyous Community*.
24. Quoted in William Braden, *The Age of Aquarius*, p. 255.
25. J. C. Furnas, *The Americans* (New York: G. P. Putnam's Sons, 1969), p. 497.
26. Noyes, *History of American Socialisms*, p. 625.
27. Spiro, *Kibbutz*, p. 114.
28. Robert Athenasiou *et al.*, "Sex," *Psychology Today*, Vol. IV, No. 2, July, 1970.
29. Robert Rimmer, *The Rebellion of Yale Marrott* (New York: Challenge, n.d.); *The Harrad Experiment* (New York: Bantam Books, Inc., 1966); *Proposition 31* (New York: New American Library, 1968).
30. See the group's statement and an account of their experiment in *Sexual Freedom*, Vol. I, No. 2, pp. 9–13.
31. David Riesman, "Individualism Reconsidered," in *Individualism Reconsidered* (Glencoe: Free Press, 1954), p. 33.

8: "*Simplify, Simplify*"

Victor Ferkiss' *Technological Man* (New York: George Braziller, Inc., 1969) and several of Lewis Mumford's books, especially *The Myth of the Machine* (New York: Harcourt, Brace & World, Inc., 1967) and *Technics and Civilization* (New York: Harcourt, Brace, 1934), are useful general discussions relevant to the themes of this chapter. On the idea of primitivism, see Arthur O. Lovejoy and George Boas *Primitivism and Related Ideas in Antiquity* (New York: Octagon Books, 1965).

1. Paul Goodman, "Rural Life: 1984," in *People or Personnel and Like a Conquered Province* (New York: Vintage Books, Inc., 1968).
2. Paul Mazur, *The Standards We Raise,* quoted in Erich

Fromm, *The Revolution of Hope* (New York: Bantam Books, Inc., 1968), p. 39.

3. Eric Hoffer, *The Ordeal of Change* (New York: Harper and Row, Publishers, 1963), pp. 23–24.
4. H. Lawrence Lack, "The Fine Art of Trashmongering," *The Mother Earth News,* November, 1970, pp. 12–13.
5. Noyes, *History of American Socialisms,* p. 19.
6. See Lynn White's "Historical Roots of Our Ecological Crisis," *Science,* March 10, 1967; Alan Watts' *Nature, Man and Woman* (New York: Random Vintage, 1970); and Theodore Roszak's *The Making of a Counter Culture,* Chapter Eight.
7. See C. P. Snow, *The Two Cultures: and a Second Look* (London: Cambridge University Press, 1964).
8. Kenneth Keniston, *The Uncommitted,* p. 429.

9: *The Search for Alternative Realities*

For a useful general discussion of the subject, see Jacob Needleman's *The New Religions* (New York: Doubleday & Company, Inc., 1971).

1. For an account of the "hexing" incident and a good general discussion, see Andrew M. Greeley's "There's a New-Time Religion on Campus," *New York Times Magazine,* June 1, 1969, p. 14 *et passim.*
2. The results of a national Gallup Poll conducted six times during the period 1957–1969 show a very consistent pattern. Americans of all faiths were asked: "At the present time, do you think religion as a whole is increasing its influence on American life or losing its influence?" Omitting the "no difference" and "no opinion" answers, the responses were as follows:

	Increasing	Losing
1957	69%	14%
1962	45	31
1965	33	45
1967	23	57
1968	18	67
1969	14	70

3. I have found two of Berger's books to be particularly useful: *The Sacred Canopy* (Garden City: Doubleday & Company, Inc., 1967) and *A Rumor of Angels* (Garden City: Doubleday & Company, Inc., 1969).

4. This comment appears in Leary's introduction to Solomon's *LSD: The Consciousness-Expanding Drug*, p. 13.

5. These are Solomon's comments in his editor's preface to *LSD: The Consciousness-Expanding Drug*.

6. See John M. Allegro's *The Sacred Mushroom and the Cross* (New York: Doubleday & Company, Inc., 1970).

7. Irving Kristol, "Urban Civilization and Its Discontents," *Commentary*, July, 1970, pp. 29–35.

8. Meher Baba, "LSD and the Highroads," *Journal of Psychedelic Drugs*, Vol. I, No. 2, 1967–68, pp. 38–44.

9. *The Modern Utopian*, Vol. II, No. 6, July, 1968, p. 31.

10. See Erikson's comments in his chapter in Erikson (ed.), *The Challenge of Youth*, pp. 1–27.

11. Ruth Benedict has written about the "vision-quest" of the Plains Indians in *Anthropologist at Work* (New York: Houghton Mifflin, 1956).

12. See Brown's article, "Apocalypse: The Place of Mystery in the Life of The Mind," *Harper's*, May, 1961. Reprinted in Mitchell Goodman (ed.), the *Movement Toward a New America*, pp. 628–630.

13. "What I Believe," *Forum*, October, 1930.

10: *Thesis, Antithesis . . . Synthesis?*

1. Jean-Francois Revel, "Without Jesus or Marx," *Saturday Review*, July 24, 1971, pp. 14–31.

2. Charles Reich, *The Greening of America* (New York: Random House, Inc., 1971).

3. Peter Drucker, "The Surprising Seventies," *Harper's*, July, 1971, pp. 35–39.

4. Kenneth Keniston, "A Second Look at the Uncommitted," *Social Policy*, July-August, 1971, pp. 6–19.

5. See Peter Berger and Brigitte Berger's comments on this point in "The Blueing of America," *Intellectual Digest*, September, 1971, pp. 25–27.

6. Chiaromonte's article appeared in *Encounter,* July, 1968, pp. 25–27. Roszak quotes these lines in *The Making of a Counter Culture,* p. 37.
7. The comment appeared in an article published in *New York Times Magazine,* February 25, 1968, p. 21 *et passim.*